The Joy of
Gluten-Free, Sugar-Free Baking

The Joy of Gluten-Free, Sugar-Free Baking

80 Low-Carb Recipes that Offer Solutions for
Celiac Disease, Diabetes, and Weight Loss

PETER REINHART & DENENE WALLACE

Photography by Leo Gong

TEN SPEED PRESS
Berkeley

Published in the United States by Ten Speed Press, an imprint of the Crown Publishing Group, a division of Random House, Inc., New York.
www.crownpublishing.com
www.tenspeed.com

Ten Speed Press and the Ten Speed Press colophon are registered trademarks of Random House, Inc.

Library of Congress Cataloging-in-Publication Data

ISBN 978-1-60774-116-9
eISBN 978-1-60774-117-6

Printed in China

Design by Katy Brown
Food styling by Karen Shinto
Prop styling by Christine Wolheim

10 9 8 7 6 5 4 3 2 1

First Edition

Contents

Foreword

When I speak to groups, I begin by telling them that at least one person in the room has experienced heart disease, kidney failure, morbid obesity, type 2 diabetes, cardiac bypass surgery, multiple vascular stents, ridiculously high cholesterol, stress-induced and explosively high blood pressure, gluten sensitivity, and cancer. I don't mean that people in the group have collectively experienced these conditions, rather that there is one individual present who has survived them all. They find it hard to believe, then I explain that it's my own health record—despite the fact that they'd never guess it since I appear to be a fit and vibrant man in his late sixties. I recount how many of my medical woes began during my fighter pilot days in Vietnam, where I experienced multiple exposures to Agent Orange. After the war, I aggressively pursued two contrapuntal paths: intensive medical study—from family practice to a specialty in surgery and another in bariatrics, plus certifications such as ABBM, FACS, and ASBP—and a self-destructive lifestyle. Ultimately, after cheating death numerous times, I began focusing on my own wellness and applied what I'd learned in my medical studies to my life.

When I met Denene Wallace, a fellow survivor of nearly fatal diabetes who had regained her health by applying a new, nutrition-based angle to her treatment, I felt like I'd met a kindred spirit. I happily consumed the many breads, cookies, and other treats she baked for me, and incorporated her dietetic approach in my own meals—which led to deeper levels of healing in my own conditions. Celiac disease, obesity, diabetes, and heart disease won't just go away; they must be managed day by day through constant self-discipline and support. That's why I am so excited that Denene joined with Peter Reinhart to share these recipes so anyone struggling with these issues can use them to build wellness.

Denene's story, which you'll read shortly, is a compelling testament to the power of being an active participant in your health management; it underpins many of the following key points on gluten intolerance, diabetes, and obesity that form the foundation of my practice.

Gluten intolerance, whether due to celiac genetic disorders or caused by other factors, often progresses from mildly annoying conditions such as colds and aches at first into a full-fledged hypersensitivity disease that requires daily vigilance. It becomes a life or death survival battle. Many symptoms of disease, such as chronic headaches, insomnia, skin rashes, and fatigue, can often be traced to gluten sensitivity even without the presence of genetic celiac disease. Eliminating or significantly reducing gluten can often alleviate these symptoms and address the condition before it becomes a full-blown disease or does further harm.

Type 2 diabetes is often an outcome of obesity, which in turn perpetuates weight problems. Obesity affects a huge proportion of the American population, and is probably the single greatest health challenge of our time. Excess weight becomes disease when the body can no longer manage the condition on its own and stops functioning as it should.

Diseases like diabetes and celiac do not go away; they must be managed. Type 2 diabetes can often be managed without insulin or medication (in conjunction with medical supervision) by adjusting the diet to eliminate excessive carbohydrates. Insulin is produced naturally in the pancreas, and its role in our body is to convert carbohydrates (and proteins, to a lesser extent) into stored fat cells, creating a reserve of emergency energy for our body. However, when we overload the pancreas and it can't keep producing insulin to deal with excessive carbs in our system, overeating morphs into the diseases of obesity and diabetes. Simple solution: get rid of the carbs to stem insulin overproduction.

The best way to reduce carbs is to stop eating the foods that contain them—especially those without fiber. On the flipside, eating foods that are high in dietary fiber is healthful in many ways, especially because they can somewhat balance out the carb load, moving carbs through the digestive system quickly and shielding the body from insulin production overload. Finally, replace high carb foods with alternatives that are high in protein. Denene and Peter have done just that, by exchanging carbohydrate- and starch-loaded flours for nut and seed flours with high amounts of protein and healthy fats.

Attaining health and wellness involves both complex and straightforward steps, but it is always simpler to deal with conditions before they become full-blown diseases. The recipes in this book provide an easy way to replace disease-causing foods with those that promote health and can even reverse the effects of disease. They will also bring you joy and well-being, which is an important part of my own formula for healing. My core belief is that while celiac, diabetes, and obesity are all diseases, the solution is not a pill. To manage or reverse them requires lifestyle changes; you have to take charge of your own body and make a commitment to a lifelong wellness path. This book is a new tool—I advise you whole heartedly to use it; it will change your life, I promise.

Dr. Tom Schneider, MD, FACS, ABBM—Healthspan Institute, Spring, 2012

Introduction

OPENING WORDS FROM PETER

I am not sensitive to gluten, as my previous books attest. However, neither am I immune to the dietary challenges brought about by the passionate consumption of products made with wheat, as anyone who has seen me also knows. There was a time when I was lean and mean, and then I opened a bakery and began a love affair with bread products of all types. Back in 1971, when I was twenty-one, I participated in a communally operated vegetarian restaurant in Boston in which no white flour, white sugar, or white rice was permitted to cross the threshold. I read everything I could find on nutrition and various popular food philosophies of the time, such as macrobiotics, raw foods and sprouts, wheat grass therapy, food combining, and juicing. I even met Jack LaLanne, one of my personal fitness heroes. For three years I ate only organically grown food and unrefined whole grains, and all of my childhood allergies and food sensitivities seemed to fade away. At five feet six inches, I weighed a lithe 136 pounds and felt great. At the end of those three years we sold the restaurant and everyone moved on, and in the next phase of my journey, I once again became an omnivore.

Even as my weight gradually increased, I maintained excellent health, which I attributed to those three dynamic years of immersion in a healthful lifestyle. By the time my wife, Susan, and I opened our own restaurant and bakery in 1986, I weighed 155 pounds and had become stocky. When we sold the business seven years later, I was up to 165 pounds and would have been heavier were it not for the daily, physically intense work of baking thousands of loaves of bread, which helped me burn off a lot of calories.

As soon as I stepped out of daily production and transitioned into teaching at culinary schools and writing books, I started gaining more weight—and quickly. The accumulated effects of tasting glorious white-flour breads of all types, along with access to the handiwork of fabulous chefs and restaurants to which I lost all ability to say no, caused my weight to balloon to over 200 pounds. Searching for the perfect pizza as I researched my book *American Pie* didn't help either, but I sure was having fun! Fortunately, I never stopped working out, so even though I was, to put it bluntly, fat, it was firm fat, marbled with muscle. Nonetheless, it was cause for concern, especially that most pernicious of fats: belly fat. So recently, with Susan's encouragement, I decided it was time to get serious about losing weight.

I had already met Denene Wallace a few years earlier at a private tasting of some of her gluten-free products and was impressed with how good they were. Gluten sensitivity is a subject I had been tracking since 1991, shortly after my first book, *Brother Juniper's Bread Book*, came out. Around that time, Loree Starr Brown, who had been a regular customer at Brother Juniper's Bakery, came in one day with a box of homemade breads and muffins based on the recipes in my book, but all made with rice flour instead of wheat flour. They were delicious. Loree proceeded to educate me about celiac disease, a medical condition that nearly killed her before it was finally diagnosed and treated by removing all traces of gluten from her diet.

At that time, it seemed that only a small number of people had issues with gluten, so there weren't many gluten-free products on the market. But like most people who stop eating bread, Loree missed it greatly, so she developed her own recipes—and then taught me the techniques she'd developed, using rice flour, tapioca flour (aka cassava flour), potato starch, xanthan gum, and egg replacers to make breads that evoked the flavors of those I made at Brother Juniper's Bakery. A few years later, Loree and I collaborated on a few gluten-free recipes that appeared in the revised *Joy of Cooking* (1998 edition), for which I served as the editor of the bread chapter. Soon I began creating my own variations of gluten-free products, employing my own trick of using flour made from sunflower seeds and pumpkin seeds to improve the flavor. One of my recipes is now used as the gluten-free crust for a major frozen food company.

The products I made were quite good—perhaps even excellent. But Denene Wallace's products were a revelation. And as every chef and gourmand knows, healthful food is really only as good as it tastes. People typically won't eat food just because it's good for them; they have to enjoy it. I believe that most of us follow what I call the "flavor rule," which, simply stated, is that flavor rules! Denene clearly adhered to this prime directive, creating baked goods of uncommon tastiness that also happened to be gluten-free, sugar-free, and low in carbohydrates, thus meeting all her dietary needs.

When the opportunity came for me to write a book about gluten-free baking—one that wouldn't simply repeat what already exists in other books but would add new options for home bakers—I decided I couldn't do it without Denene as my coauthor. So we brought together our collective knowledge and the fruits of our experimentation to present more than eighty recipes unlike any that exist in other books and that, in our opinion, are not just safe for those who must avoid gluten, sugar, and foods with a high glycemic index, but also are so delicious that even those who don't have such dietary restrictions will embrace them. After all, flavor rules!

To take my commitment one step further, I had a personal objective when working on this book. Unlike the process of creating my previous books, in which I gained weight during the recipe testing, this time I wanted to lose weight—at least 25 pounds and hopefully more, by the time it came out. I'll report on that later, in the Epilogue.

OPENING WORDS FROM DENENE

I've always felt that I was an artist at heart, even in childhood. My artistic inclinations were evident in my love for drawing and my seemingly constant desire to rearrange and redecorate my bedroom. These talents eventually led to a very successful career in interior design, first in Louisiana, then in Georgia. In the early 1990s, I established my own interior design studio, The Design Source, in a suburb of Atlanta. For fifteen years, I thoroughly enjoyed building my business by creating beautiful living environments for my clients.

Little did I know that my creativity and artistic skills would eventually serve me well in an entirely different realm: dealing with an unexpected and life-changing health issue. First, my husband, Greg, and I discovered that we were both gluten sensitive in 2003. Then, in the summer of 2006, my doctor told me that I had type 2 diabetes and would require insulin shots for the rest of my life. The news was devastating. I'd never had a weight problem and always thought of myself as quite healthy. I began a regimen of five insulin shots a day and also started educating myself about diabetes. My research led me to believe that changing my diet and exercise habits might allow me to at least reduce the number of insulin shots, and possibly eliminate the need for them entirely.

As I educated myself on blood sugar issues, I began to eliminate various foods from my diet. Removing products containing sugar was relatively easy because I had never been a big eater of sweets or desserts. The challenge was drastically reducing my intake of carbohydrates, which are digested into sugars that ultimately enter the bloodstream. Reducing or eliminating starches such as rice, potatoes, and corn was difficult but achievable. However, I struggled with removing all grain-based bread products from my diet. Living on meat, green vegetables, and salads simply wasn't enough for a Southern girl raised on Mama's home cooking. I searched supermarkets, natural food stores, and the Internet for alternative products I could consume without a negative impact on my blood sugar levels. But what I found was downright depressing. The grain-free products available at the time tasted like cardboard or worse.

I eventually realized that in order to have bread products that I not only could eat, but actually *wanted* to eat, I would probably need to make my own. So I began experimenting with alternative flours. The process was long, tedious, and punctuated with many failures that ended up in the trash can. Because I had no formal training as a baker, my learning curve was rather steep. However, my lack of training also had a huge benefit: I didn't have any preconceived notions or rules to block my creative explorations, especially with nut and seed flours. After two years and a multitude of baking experiments, Proseed Flour was born, along with a line of baked goods that now consists of more than fifty products—all absolutely delicious. By substituting these products for conventional grain-based baked goods (along with other diet and lifestyle changes), I was actually able to eliminate my need for insulin shots completely.

I'm currently in the process of licensing Proseed Flour products to major food companies. As part of the early process to determine the appropriate markets for these products, our marketing firm, Davis Brand Capital, brought in Peter Reinhart for a taste test. Peter was extremely impressed with the taste and texture of the eight different products that Greg and I presented that day and said that he thought I had achieved new heights in baking with alternative flours. Later, when he was given the opportunity to write a gluten-free baking book for Ten Speed Press, he said, "Let's go all the way and make it gluten-free, sugar-free, and low-carb" and invited me to be his coauthor.

Although I've had no formal training as a baker or chef, I've always considered myself an excellent Southern cook, and I've always enjoyed creating delicious meals for family and friends. Rest assured that I was equally determined to develop delicious recipes for this book—recipes every bit as good as those using my Proseed Flour. In addition, I wanted to be sure that the recipes are simple enough to be easily duplicated and accessible to people without formal training. Each recipe was developed and tested under Peter's guidance.

The gluten-free, low-carb alternative flours in these recipes have changed my life and helped heal my body. My hope is that this book becomes an effective tool for those who require an alternative diet, as well as for those who just want great-tasting, healthy baked products. I believe that everyone should eat food that tastes great, and it is even better when great-tasting food is also great for you. Enjoy!

ABOUT THIS BOOK

These recipes are designed to meet the dietary needs of people who are sensitive to gluten or have diabetic or prediabetic conditions. There are only small amounts of carbohydrates in most of these recipes, mostly from the nut and seed flours and small amounts of fruit or vegetables. In all of these cases, the carbs are balanced out by the complementary natural fiber in these foods. These are baked goods that have essentially no glycemic load, making it possible for people with blood sugar or insulin concerns to enjoy them freely.

The secret to the success of the recipes in this book is twofold: utilizing a variety of nut and seed flours, and working with alternative, sugar-free sweeteners. You'll learn all about these ingredients in the chapter "The Basics." Be sure to read the pantry section, as it provides details on how to make your own nut and seed flours, as well as why we mostly use certain alternative sweeteners (and why you need to do the same). Once you've digested that information, you'll be able to join us in creating the most unique and delicious gluten-free, sugar-free, low-carb baked goods you've ever had. As a bonus, these baked goods are not only safe for diabetics and people with gluten sensitivity, but also a good choice for many folks who are looking for a healthful alternative to traditional baked goods. Barring allergies to nuts or other ingredients we call for, these recipes are a perfect fit for anyone on a low-carb diet, such as Atkins, South Beach, the Belly Fat Cure, Sugar Busters, and others, and are also a healthy alternative for kids' lunch boxes.

Obviously, there is no one diet that works for everyone. If you're allergic or sensitive to tree nuts, these recipes won't work for you. Fortunately, there are plenty of specialized cookbooks available, including some with a focus on allergen-free recipes (we've listed our favorites in the Resources section). Our mission here is to serve the large and, unfortunately, growing population of people with diabetes, prediabetes, weight loss and obesity struggles, and gluten intolerance. If the innovative recipes in this book accomplish this by offering you new and delicious options, it will be a very good day for us.

These baked goods do, of course, contain calories; however, when used to replace your normal, starch-based baked goods, they will actually help with weight loss. These recipes are free of calories from the sugars and refined grains typically used in baked goods—considered to be "empty" calories because they contain minimal nutrients beyond their carbohydrate. Sugars and refined grains are also rapidly converted into blood sugar (glucose), and if they aren't quickly burned up by activity, they're eventually stored as fat.

We believe that everyone will love these recipes, even people without dietary restrictions. It's true that the baked goods they yield won't taste like those made with wheat. For that matter, they also won't taste like gluten-free baked goods made with rice and tapioca flour—and we view this as a good thing! They have their own distinctive flavor and texture, and we believe that they are extremely delicious and will please your palate. And regardless of dietary restrictions, most folks could benefit from eating fewer sugars and refined carbs, and from introducing more variety into their diet. This book will help you do just that.

All of that said, we imagine you've chosen this cookbook because you or someone you love has issues with sugar, gluten, obesity, or carbohydrates. If so, you're probably well aware of all of the ins and outs of these medical conditions. However, if you have further questions about these topics, the Resources section will point you toward some reputable sources of information. Just to be clear, we aren't making any health claims or offering a dietary plan in this book. That's a job for the experts, and we're happy to refer you to them. However, we will give you just a bit of background information on food allergies, gluten sensitivity, obesity, and diabetic considerations in the sections that follow.

Allergy Considerations

This is not an allergen-free cookbook. Anyone who has tree nut allergies will not be able to eat the baked goods in this book—sorry. Dairy intolerance shouldn't be an issue, as there are many alternative milks widely available and all work well in these recipes. Our goal is to provide a resource for people who are sensitive to gluten or have difficulty with sugar and carbs. Again, if food allergies prevent you from using the recipes in this book, see the Resources section, where we've listed several cookbooks written to accommodate other food sensitivities.

Wheat and Gluten Considerations

Gluten sensitivity, which can range from slight reactions to a life-threatening condition, is becoming an increasingly common issue. Though we won't get into the details, we do think it's helpful to outline some terms and distinctions. *Wheat intolerance,* which is fairly common, lies at the mild end of the spectrum and refers to difficulties digesting wheat. Common symptoms include bloating, diarrhea, and fatigue. Depending on the level of wheat intolerance, people may be able to tolerate limited amounts of wheat or wheat hybrids such as spelt if eaten infrequently.

Wheat allergy refers to an actual allergic reaction to wheat, which, when severe, may cause anaphylactic shock; this is obviously life-threatening—but also relatively uncommon, occurring in less than 0.5 percent of the U.S. population. Those with genuine wheat allergies must avoid eating any foods containing wheat or wheat hybrids.

Finally, *gluten intolerance* refers to celiac disease, a serious autoimmune disorder of the small intestine that affects less than 1 percent of the U.S. population. It occurs in people of all ages and has a strong genetic component. Symptoms of celiac disease are often similar to those of wheat intolerance and include chronic diarrhea and fatigue. However, symptoms may not manifest until an accumulation of exposure causes a major health crisis. At that point, symptoms are typically numerous and unpleasant at best. In addition, those with celiac disease are more likely to suffer from a host of other medical conditions, from other autoimmune conditions to intestinal cancer to diabetes.

Celiac disease is caused by a reaction to wheat proteins, mainly gliadin (a component of gluten), creating severe bowel disorders that result in general malnutrition and constant inflammation. The only known treatment for celiac disease is complete avoidance of gluten.

Diabetic Considerations

Our objective when creating these recipes was to keep the carbohydrate content as low as possible. Denene uses carb counting to assess quantities of net carbohydrates. We'll assume that you're familiar with carb counting. If you aren't you can read up on it at www.nal.usda .gov/fnic/foodcomp/search or www.nutritionvalue.org. The key to calculating net carbs is to subtract the total fiber from the total carbohydrates (usually in grams). The result is the net carbs. The lower the net carbs, the lower the glycemic load. All of our recipes have 10 net carbs or less per serving, and most have far fewer. For example, Toasting Bread (page 34) has 1 net carb per serving. Note that this is only true of the recipes as written, using alternative sweeteners, unsweetened applesauce and soy milk, and minimal amounts of fruit. The low number of net carbs also relies on using full-fat dairy products. If you substitute reduced-fat ingredients, there will be less fat to buffer whatever carbs the final product does contain, so the effect on blood sugar is likely to be greater.

The Role of Glucose
Simply stated, glucose (aka blood sugar) is sugar that our bodies convert into energy. It falls into the category of simple sugars (monosaccharides), which are the basic building blocks of all carbohydrates. Its root word in ancient Greek, *glukus*, means "sweet." It provides many positive functions for us (like fueling the brain!), but it is also at the root of diabetes, a disease that's reaching epidemic proportions in the United States and many other countries. The causes and mechanisms of diabetes and related conditions are far too complicated to

explain here, but we will give a brief overview. Insulin, a hormone produced in the pancreas, helps the body use or store excess glucose in the bloodstream. In a healthy body, blood sugar levels increase slightly after a meal, then the pancreas releases insulin to keep blood sugar levels within a normal range. If blood sugar levels get too high, this can cause all sorts of damage to the body, especially to the eyes, kidneys, and, eventually, the heart.

The bottom line is that elevated blood glucose levels are often a sign of diabetes or prediabetes and cause for concern. If you suspect that you have issues with blood sugar levels, including hypoglycemia (abnormally low blood sugar levels), you should seek testing immediately. Your doctor will know which test to administer. And whether or not you have diabetic or prediabetic issues, if your diet is anything like that of most Americans, you're probably consuming too many carbs, which ultimately means too much glucose.

Glycemic Index and Glycemic Load

Glycemic index (GI) is a rating of the effect of foods that contain carbohydrates on blood sugar levels. Specifically, the rating is based on how quickly the carbohydrates break down during digestion and how rapidly they release glucose into the bloodstream. The more quickly they release glucose into the bloodstream, the higher their GI. Foods with a low GI release glucose more slowly and steadily, while those with a high GI cause a more rapid rise in blood sugar levels. Most diabetics now have a pretty good understanding of the glycemic index, as do those who have followed various diet programs like the South Beach Diet, Sugar Busters, or the Belly Fat Cure. It's a helpful tool for keeping blood sugar and insulin levels under control. (There are links to reliable sources for more information on this subject in the Resources section.)

Glycemic load (GL) is a way to rank the carb content in foods by considering both portion size and the food's glycemic index rating. This helps you know how that portion will impact your blood sugar levels. The formula used to determine glycemic load is GI multiplied by the amount of available carbohydrates, divided by 100. (Available carbohydrates are measured in grams and exclude indigestible fiber.) Multiplying the glycemic index by the amount of carbohydrates in a serving of food gives a better idea of the effect of that serving on blood sugar levels. For example, a 100-gram serving of a piece of fruit with a GI of 70 and a carbohydrate content of 6 grams results in the calculation 70 x 6 = 420; when divided by 100, that's a GL of 4.2.

The presence of fat or fiber slows the release of glucose into the bloodstream and can therefore lower the overall glycemic load. Our goal in this book was to create recipes that have a very low GL so they won't have an adverse effect on blood sugar, making them accessible

Tip: Getting Good Carbs

Even if you do have issues with blood sugar and insulin, you still need some carbs to round out a healthful diet. So where can you get them? The simple answer is to eat lots of fresh vegetables and fruit. However, some fruits are more problematic for diabetics than others. For instance, berries and pitted fruits like cherries, plums, and peaches are generally a better choice than sweeter tropical fruits, like bananas and pineapple. However, this type of sensitivity varies from person to person, especially regarding appropriate portion sizes. In any case, we want to be clear that we aren't nutritionists or health professionals. Be sure to work with a qualified physician, preferably one who is well versed in nutrition (sadly, not all are), to determine what works best for you.

to people with insulin and blood sugar issues. However, do bear in mind that GI and GL are just tools; every person is different, and there is no single dietary approach that is right for everyone. If you are diabetic, you probably know more about this topic than we provided in this brief explanation, and hopefully you are working with a doctor to manage your condition.

Naturally Occurring Sugars

If you're at all savvy about nutrition, you're probably wondering about whether baking with fruit is an issue. After all, fruit contains sugar. This is a valid concern. Adding fruit does add sugars and carbs (the same is true of many vegetables). But sugars that come as part of a whole food, such as raisins, cranberries, apples, or sweet potatoes, are accompanied by fiber, protein, and many other nutrients in that whole food, and this tends to lessen the glycemic impact and effect on blood sugar levels. Still, because our goal is to give you recipes with minimal glycemic load, we aren't heavy-handed with fruit, using it only in selected recipes and only in small amounts. If insulin and blood sugar levels aren't an issue for you, feel free to increase the amount of fruit or vegetables in these recipes. (In fact, you can even replace the sugar substitutes with regular sugar if you are so inclined; we'll discuss this in greater detail in the pantry section.)

The Basics

In this chapter, we'll discuss ingredients that we call for frequently or that are unusual and also explain how to make nut and seed flours. We'll also outline the equipment you'll need in a tutorial showing basic mixing and baking methods that apply to nearly every recipe in this book. The recipes are actually quite easy to make, so once you've read through this section, you'll be able to jump right in and start whipping up your own homemade treats. In fact, the recipes are so easy to make that you can jump in without reading any of the introductory sections—except for the material on making your own nut and seed flours on page 13, which is a must. Still, we think the information in this chapter will prove both helpful and interesting, so we encourage you to read all of it. Of course, over time new information will become available and new recipes will arise, so we've created a website where we can share new recipes and techniques and also answer questions: www.thejoyofgluten-freesugar-freebaking.com.

THE GLUTEN-FREE, SUGAR-FREE PANTRY

Some of the ingredients you will need for the recipes in this book are fairly typical and may already be in your pantry or refrigerator. You may need to purchase others, and there are some that you'll have to make yourself. (Not to worry: Doing so is easy, and we'll explain how in this section.) For the ingredients that are available commercially, many are available at well-stocked natural food stores and even supermarkets, and if not, they are available online or by mail order (see the Resources section or our website for suppliers).

A few years ago hardly anyone knew about almond flour; now, thanks to gluten-free cookbooks by authors like Elana Amsterdam, it has worked its way into the mainstream. That's a great start. Now, in this book, we're going to stretch the boundaries and utilize flours made from a wide variety of other nuts and seeds. The alternative flours we use most often are almond, coconut, hazelnut, pecan, and sesame seed, along with flaxseed meal. Only a few of these are commercially available, typically almond flour, coconut flour, hazelnut flour, and flaxseed meal; pecan flour is available from some producers but is hard to find. (And note that they may be labeled "meal," not "flour," as in "almond meal.") Bob's Red Mill makes all of these flours, along with a wide variety of other gluten-free products, and these are generally available in well-stocked markets—and always available online. In the next section, we'll give you precise instructions for making all of the alternative flours.

Of course, alternative sweeteners also play a huge role in these recipes. And because we know many readers may have other dietary considerations, we've made these recipes flexible in regard to ingredients like butter, milk, and eggs. So, yes, in addition to being gluten-free and low in carbohydrates, essentially all of these recipes are vegan-friendly. (By the way, if you have trouble finding any of the commercially available ingredients, check out the Resources section on page 208. And, as new sources emerge, we'll list them on our website.)

Alternative Flours

In addition to almond, coconut, hazelnut, pecan, and sesame seed flour and flaxseed meal, we sometimes call for flours made from pumpkin seeds, sunflower seeds, walnuts, and even garbanzo beans (chickpeas). And as you will see, many of the recipes have variations that involve using different types of flour. All of the nut and seed flours are interchangeable, and the possible combinations are almost endless. We encourage you to use the recipes in this book as a template for experimentation. Play with the flours and combinations and discover what qualities different flours impart and which blends you like best. You can also substitute flours made from other nuts, such as pistachios, macadamia nuts, and even peanuts.

We recognize that nuts and seeds and the flours made from them are more costly than flours made from grains (and legumes). This is unfortunate, but we believe the payoff in terms of flavor is well worth the expense. And if you've had to avoid bread and baked goods because of dietary concerns, you'll probably consider the expense justified. Even so, you can considerably reduce the expense by buying nuts and seeds in bulk and making your own flours. For example, a pound of almonds is about half the price of a pound of almond flour. This difference can add up quickly. In the long run, if your choice is between store-bought "dietetic" foods, we believe making your own breads and other treats at home won't be significantly more expensive—but will be immensely more delicious!

If making nut and seed flours at home, simply purchase the nuts or seeds in whole form and then grind them until powdery, as described on page 13. Sometimes almond flour is made from blanched almonds; however, for these recipes, that isn't necessary. Likewise, hazelnuts need not be skinned before grinding them into flour. In both cases, the skins add fiber and nutrients, and that's a good thing. That said, you can certainly use almond flour from blanched almonds if you prefer or if that's what you have on hand.

If you can purchase nuts and seeds in bulk at a store with a high turnover rate, that's your best bet. That way they will be fresh and you can buy just a pound or two at a time, as needed. If you order by mail, you may need to buy larger quantities. Either way, store the nuts and seeds in an airtight container—preferably in the freezer if you have room, or in the refrigerator. They will keep for months. This is especially true for coconut flour and pecan flour, which have a strong tendency to dry out if not stored in airtight containers.

One last consideration about working with nut and seed flours: Just as with wheat flour, some brands of almond or pecan flour may be drier than others, and the almond and other nut flours you make at home may also have a different moisture content. Because of these natural variations, the consistency of a dough or batter may not be as described in the recipe. (This can also occur because of inaccurate measuring, using different sizes of eggs, and so on.) Begin with the quantities of ingredients called for in the recipe, but pay close attention to the descriptions of how various mixtures and the final product should appear and what they should feel like. If a mixture seems too dry to form it into the proper shape, it's fine to add more liquid as needed. Likewise, if a mixture seems too wet, feel free to add a bit more nut or seed flour to reach the right consistency.

We have found that the greatest discrepancy can occur when using commercially ground pecan flour instead of home ground, and when using coconut flour that has been left open to the air and has dried out further—in both cases the flour will absorb more liquid than normal. In some instances, the amount of extra liquid needed to reach the proper consistency can be as much as an additional ¼ cup per every cup of pecan flour (beyond the amount specified in the recipe). But because the degree of discrepancy is difficult to predict, in every recipe we describe what the batter should feel and look like; use these cues to guide your adjustments.

One of the joys of working with nut and seed flours is that the recipes are very flexible and tolerant of such adjustments—which often isn't the case for recipes made with conventional flour and yeast. The truth is, if a batter or dough is too wet, the recipe will probably turn out just fine. It may take longer to bake than the instructions indicate, but that could also happen if your oven is inaccurate. The key to success is to pay attention to the descriptions in the method, adjust the batter or dough accordingly, and use the visual and textural cues as your primary guide in determining doneness.

Making Nut and Seed Flours

If you have a seed or coffee grinder, making your own nut and seed flours is easy, though you may have to make several small batches to produce the amount needed for a recipe. (You can also use a food processor or blender, as described below.) If you'll be making nut and seed flours often, we recommend investing in a good-quality seed grinder. They typically accommodate about ½ cup (120 ml) of seeds (about 1.75 oz / 50 g) or nuts (about 2 oz / 57 g). (For pointers on making coconut flour, see the Tip on page 14; for garbanzo bean flour, see the Tip on page 38, though it is now available already ground at most natural foods markets.) Pulse a few times and then grind continuously for about 5 seconds. Remove the lid and check on the consistency. If the flour is still unevenly ground, stir it with a spoon or a small spatula to break it up and get it off the grinder wall, then grind for a few more seconds. Here's the most important point: *Don't grind any longer than it takes to create a fine meal. If you do, you run the risk of making nut or seed butter, not flour.* Repeat the process until you have enough flour for the recipe.

A food processor with the metal blade attachment also works well but typically can't grind flour as finely as a seed or coffee grinder can. However, you can grind a larger amount at once—often the full amount needed for recipe. With the exception of coconut, these

Tip: Making Coconut Flour

Bob's Red Mill and a few other companies make coconut flour, so you can purchase it if you like. If it isn't available locally, you can buy it online. Or, as with nut and seed flours, you can make it at home. Simply grind unsweetened coconut flakes into a flour in a spice or seed grinder. Better yet, toast the coconut first (see Tip, page 150). In addition to making the coconut easier to grind, toasting also gives the flour a deeper coconut flavor that nicely enhances many baked goods.

alternative flours are more voluminous than the ingredients they're made from. A good starting point is to use about three-fourths the volume of the amount of flour you want to make. So for 1 cup of almond flour, you might start with ¾ cup of almonds. Process the nuts or seeds for about 10 seconds and then remove the lid to check the consistency. Continue grinding as needed, using short pulses rather than an extended period of processing, until the flour has an even consistency. Again, be careful not to process the flour too long, or you may end up with a paste.

Using a blender takes some trial and error. Be careful not to overload the blender, as the nuts or seeds on the bottom will get packed under those above. This may happen anyway, so it's a good idea to process for just a few seconds at a time and then stir to redistribute. Depending on the size of your blender, about 1 cup (240 ml) of seeds (3.5 oz / 99 g) or nuts (4 oz / 113 g) will probably be about the maximum for each batch. Blend at low speed to avoid creating too much friction and heat, which create nut or seed butter, rather than flour. If the ingredients are mostly ground into a flour but some larger particles remain, that's fine. Just use the flour as is; that way you'll avoid creating a paste—and the final baked good will simply have more crunch.

Flours Made from Gluten-Free Grains, Beans, and Other Alternatives

We've chosen to build our recipes around nut and seed flours, rather than flours made from beans and gluten-free grains, for two main reasons: glycemic load and flavor. Many grains and grainlike seeds are gluten-free and commonly available as flours (amaranth, buckwheat, corn, millet, quinoa, rice, sorghum, teff, wild rice, and, possibly, oats). They typically have good flavor, along with good nutritional value if used in whole-grain form. However, all are composed primarily of carbohydrates and therefore contribute significantly to the glycemic load, causing blood sugar spikes (whole grains less so than refined grains). If you can tolerate carbs from gluten-free grains, then by all means use them in your baked goods. There are numerous excellent cookbooks to guide you in doing so, and we've recommended a few in the Resources section.

Flours made from beans and legumes, such as black beans, fava beans, garbanzo beans, lentils, and the like, are very nutritious, but they are often difficult to digest and also aren't nearly as tasty as nut and seed flours. Plus, legumes have a considerable carbohydrate component, and some people find that flours made from them have a significant negative effect on blood sugar levels. However, in our experience garbanzo bean flour doesn't have as pronounced an effect, so we've used it in a few recipes. If you don't have problems with bean flours, feel free to experiment with substituting them for some of the flour we call for in these recipes. We recommend starting with relatively modest amounts—perhaps no more than 25 percent of the flour called for in a recipe.

Beyond legumes and gluten-free grains, many other foods can be used to make flour. A few examples are tapioca starch, potato flour, and even mesquite beans. But, again, we feel that nut and seed flours produce the tastiest results without negative glycemic loads, so those are the flours we've focused on.

Sweeteners

The second major way in which these recipes deviate from those for traditional baked goods is using commercially available sugar replacers. Obviously, we cannot include sugar in recipes for people with blood sugar issues, nor can we use alternative sugars, from agave syrup to maple syrup to Sucanat—all contain sugars, and all have a high glycemic index. Yet, as many home bakers know, artificial sweeteners like Sweet'N Low and Equal don't perform well in baked goods because they are so concentrated that they don't caramelize, and caramelization is an essential aspect of proper crust and flavor development. Our sweeteners of choice are Splenda (sucralose) and stevia, which is totally natural and derived from a plant. However, pure stevia, when used alone, is so concentrated that it can't supply the bulk and caramelizing qualities required. We do call for liquid stevia extract, however, to boost the sweet flavor, and also offer a couple of stevia-based sweeteners as an alternative to Splenda, which we'll discuss first.

Splenda (or, more precisely, Splenda No Calorie Sweetener) is a commercial product designed to be substituted for sugar on a one-for-one basis. It is a combination of sucralose and maltodextrin, and performs well in these recipes. Numerous studies have indicated that sucralose is safe in the quantities usually ingested. Feel free to use it in these recipes, as it really does taste and perform like sugar. Be sure to purchase the granulated version, which is formulated for baking. Most supermarkets now offer generic versions of Splenda, which perform the same and can save you money.

For those who prefer not to use Splenda, fortunately, stevia is also available as Stevia Extract in the Raw, an excellent sugar substitute that employs stevia for sweetness. The cup-for-cup version of Stevia Extract in the Raw, specifically formulated for baking and cooking, is made by combining an extract from the leaves of the stevia plant with maltodextrin, which is enzymatically derived from either corn or wheat. In the United States, maltodextrin is typically made from corn, and that is the source of the maltodextrin in Stevia Extract in the Raw. (If you're sensitive to gluten, take note: In the United Kingdom maltodextrin is often made from wheat; however, the processing is so extensive that, according to the manufacturers, no gluten remains—so all maltodextrin is, at least theoretically, gluten-free.) Maltodextrin is a carbohydrate, and it is absorbed into the bloodstream as sugar is, but adds less than 1 gram of carbs per serving (Stevia Extract in the Raw contains even less, only ½ gram) and is balanced out by the fiber in the nut and seed flours.

Another product that works well is a blend of stevia extract powder and fructooligosaccharides derived from vegetable sources (fructooligosaccharides have a sweet flavor but are essentially indigestible fiber). One such product is New Roots Stevia Sugar. Note that it is more concentrated than Stevia Extract in the Raw, so the recipes in this book call for half the amount of sweetener if using New Roots Stevia Sugar instead of Splenda or Stevia Extract in the Raw. One downside to New Roots Stevia Sugar is that it's quite expensive and available mainly through mail order. Despite these downsides, we include it here because it's more widely available in the United Kingdom, whereas Stevia Extract in the Raw was only recently approved.

We tried several other sugar replacers, such as Truvia, Z-Sweet, and Organic Zero. These are all excellent products, but they all use erythritol for bulking. As a result, they tend to melt too quickly for thin products like cookies, scones, and pancakes. However, they do work well in cakes. If you choose to experiment with using these sweeteners, do so selectively, and study the equivalencies carefully. For example, Z-Sweet and Organic Zero can replace sugar (or Splenda or Stevia Extract in the Raw) in equal quantities, whereas if using Truvia, the amount needed would be less—closer to the amount of New Roots Stevia Sugar called for. These erythritol-based sweeteners work especially well in certain contexts, like toppings and glazes, and where they do, the ingredient list offers the option of using them.

We experimented with making our own sugar replacers using erythritol (an essentially non-caloric sugar alcohol that doesn't affect blood sugar levels), polydextrose (a sweet, indigestible soluble fiber), and other such ingredients, but we found that none of them performed as well in these recipes as either Splenda or Stevia Extract in the Raw. Plus, some of those ingredients can be difficult to come by, whereas Splenda and Stevia Extract in the Raw can both be found in most American supermarkets.

In the end, we settled on three products that work in all of our recipes for baked goods: Splenda (or supermarket-brand Splenda generics), Stevia Extract in the Raw, and New Roots Stevia Sugar. Splenda is widely available and New Roots Stevia Sugar is available by mail order in the United States and the United Kingdom. Because we believe that many readers will be using Stevia Extract in the Raw, which we hope will become more internationally available by the time this book is published, or Splenda, we have written the measurements for these products. But for those using New Roots Stevia Sugar or similar brands, you will need to use half the amount, as indicated in the recipes.

You'll note that the measurements for the sugar replacers are given in volume only, not in weights. While weights are generally more accurate than volume measurements, sugar replacers typically rely on a highly concentrated sweetener combined with a bulking agent, and their weight-to-volume ratios vary widely. In all cases, they are much lighter, cup for cup, than sugar. If sugar isn't an issue for you and you wish to use it when baking, simply substitute the same volume of sugar as indicated for Splenda and Stevia Extract in the Raw.

One final note: We also call for liquid stevia extract in a few of the recipes to boost the sweetness without throwing off the balance of ingredients needed to create a final product with good texture and caramelization. Liquid stevia is highly concentrated—just a few drops is equal to a teaspoon of sugar—so it isn't used in large volumes. The amounts we call for are usually less than 1 teaspoon. Liquid stevia, for sale under the Sweet Leaf and NOW brands, is available at almost any natural foods market. However, it is relatively expensive in stores, so refer to our Resources section for a mail order option that greatly reduces the cost.

Baking Powder

Most of the recipes in this book rely on baking powder and eggs for leavening. (A few use baking soda.) Where we call for yeast, it's included for flavor only, not leavening, as there are so few carbs available to feed the yeast. Baking powder often contains some starch to absorb moisture and stabilize the mixture. Unfortunately, that bit of starch may (though rarely) be derived from wheat, so people who are highly sensitive to gluten may react to commercial baking powder. If this is an issue for you, you can make your own baking powder by combining two parts cream of tartar with one part baking soda. We recommend making up a small batch; for example, combining ½ cup (2.5 oz / 71 g) cream of tartar with ¼ cup (1.75 oz / 50 g) baking soda. Simply whisk them together until thoroughly combined, breaking up any lumps with your fingers. Store your homemade baking powder in an airtight container in a cool, dry place. If it absorbs any moisture, it will lose it's leavening power, which is one reason why we recommend that you make it in small batches. It's easy to make more when you need it.

This combination of cream of tartar and baking soda is what is known as single-acting baking powder. As soon as the ingredients get wet, they contribute leavening due to a chemical process in which the acidity, or low pH, of the cream of tartar reacts with the high pH, or alkalinity, of the baking soda, releasing carbon dioxide in the process, and thereby causing baked goods to rise. Because this reaction begins as soon as the ingredients get wet, you need to bake products made with single-acting baking powder as soon as possible.

Commercial double-acting baking powder contains a second acid that doesn't activate until it's exposed to high temperatures, creating a second phase of leavening. If, like most people, you aren't sensitive to commercial, double-acting baking powder, you can use it in all of these recipes.

Butter, Margarine, and Vegetable Oils

Most of these recipes call for salted butter. This was a tough call for us because professional bakers always prefer to work with unsalted butter. But because many of our readers may be vegans or may wish to avoid butter for a variety of reasons, we offer the option of replacing the butter with a butter substitute, such as Smart Balance (or other natural margarines), and these almost always contain salt. Therefore, we formulated these recipes to use salted butter.

This also explains why some of the recipes have so little added salt: some salt is already included in the butter or margarine. If you use unsalted butter or margarine, simply increase the amount of salt as follows:

- For ¼ cup or less of butter, don't adjust the amount of salt.

- For amounts of butter between ¼ cup and ¾ cup, add an additional ¼ teaspoon salt.

- For ¾ cup to 1 cup of butter, add an additional ½ teaspoon salt.

If you choose to use margarine, we recommend Smart Balance or Earth Balance. Both are interchangeable with butter. These recipes were primarily tested using butter, but when we did test with margarine, we chose Smart Balance Original Flavor Buttery Spread. If you use a different brand, please read the label closely and be sure to avoid any that contain hydrogenated oils. Hydrogenated oils (aka trans fats) are associated with a risk for certain health conditions (possibly including type 2 diabetes), so we advise that you steer clear of these.

You can also substitute any type of vegetable oil, but it's a more complex proposition, because oil contains more fat and less water than salted butter and margarine—and of course no salt.

If the recipe calls for this much salted butter	Substitute this much vegetable oil	This much water	And this much salt
¼ cup	3 tablespoons	1 tablespoon	none
½ cup	6 tablespoons	2 tablespoons	¼ teaspoon
¾ cup	½ cup plus 1 tablespoon	3 tablespoons	½ teaspoon
1 cup	¾ cup	¼ cup	½ teaspoon

We prefer cold-pressed corn, canola, or safflower oil. That said, choose the oil you prefer and that's best for your own body's needs. Just two caveats: Don't substitute oil for the salted butter or margarine in recipes calling for lemon juice. There's a synergy to the combination of lemon and buttery flavors that will be missing if you substitute vegetable oil. Also, use olive oil only when specified. We recommend saving flavorful (and more costly) extra-virgin olive oil for savory toppings and using regular olive oil in the doughs.

Eggs

Whenever we call for eggs we mean large eggs, not extra large or medium. A typical large egg weighs about 1.65 to 1.75 ounces (47 to 50 g). We use 1.75 oz (50 g) as the standard. It's fine to substitute liquid eggs or an egg replacer for the eggs in a recipe. Be sure to check the ingredients list carefully though, as some brands of egg replacer contain gluten or starch. If you use liquid eggs, use the weight of eggs called for in the ingredients list. If using a powdered egg replacer, reconstitute it according to the instructions to equal the number of eggs called for; use it as a wet ingredient, not a dry ingredient.

For recipes that call for egg whites only, we recommend that you buy liquid egg whites rather than separating eggs. Not only are they inexpensive and easy to use, but this also avoids the dilemma of what to do with all of the extra yolks. Some powdered egg replacers, such as Ener-G brand, also have instructions for using the product in place of egg whites.

Note that you can't use egg replacers for egg washes. If you prefer not to use an egg wash, which functions primarily to create a shine on the surface of the finished product, you can either omit it altogether or brush a small amount of vegetable oil on the surface of the baked item as soon as it comes out of the oven to create the sheen.

Also, you can't use egg replacer powders in place of egg whites beaten to soft or stiff peaks, which a few recipes call for. In those instances you can still make the recipe, but the results won't be as light and lofty. You can, however, mix the batter longer to create as much aeration as possible to compensate for the absence of the egg foam.

Milk

Whenever milk is called for, you can use any kind you wish, as long as it's sugar-free or unsweetened. Even if you don't have issues with sugar, you need to use unsweetened milk because that's how the recipes are formulated, so sweetened products will affect the final flavor. Other than that consideration, choose from cow's milk, goat's milk, or nondairy milks made from soy, almonds, coconut, or hemp seeds, depending on your dietary needs or taste preferences. All work equally well in these recipes, where the function of the milk is to tenderize the dough and contribute additional nutrients. If you prefer, you can even substitute water for the milk, though the final product may not be quite as tasty. You will see that unsweetened soy milk is often listed as the suggested choice; this is because it adds no net carbs to a recipe, which will be especially helpful to those whose concern is more focused on the glycemic issues rather than the gluten-free aspect.

One word of caution in regard to reduced-fat milk: We believe that people with severe problems with blood sugar control should generally steer clear of reduced-fat milk and dairy products. Though it may seem odd, milk does contain carbs (primarily in the form of the sugar lactose). The fat in whole milk helps balance the glycemic load from these carbs. But as we've said elsewhere, everyone is different, and we understand that for some folks other dietary issues may make full-fat milk products inadvisable. Again, choose the form of milk that works best for you and your body, and that best supports your health.

Other Ingredients

Butter-flavored sprinkles: This may seem like an unusual ingredient, but they're widely available—and essential for our pretzels! We also call for them in a few other recipes. You can find them at almost any supermarket. Look for them in the area where spices or baking ingredients are stocked.

Cheese: As discussed in regard to milk, we believe that people with severe problems with blood sugar control should generally steer clear of reduced-fat dairy products, including cheese. Nondairy cheeses, such as Galaxy Nutritional Soy Cheese brand Veggie Slices or shredded cheese, can be used in any recipe calling for cheese. These soy and other nondairy cheeses now come in a variety of styles, including mozzarella, Cheddar, pepper Jack, and Swiss.

Chocolate: There are a number of sugar-free semi-sweet chocolate bars and baking chips on the market. We think ChocoPerfection is by far the tastiest sugar-free chocolate (see Resources). Unfortunately, it doesn't come in chips (it did at one time but was no longer available at the time of publication, though this could change), but you can always buy the bars and chop them up. However, most brands of sugar-free chocolate should perform just fine in these recipes.

Cocoa powder: Most of our recipes will work with either standard cocoa powder (also called natural cocoa) or European cocoa (also called Dutched or Dutch-process). Some recipes specifically call for European cocoa, which means that the cocoa has been alkalized to make it darker and taste less acidic, because we prefer that flavor in the recipe. However, you can use regular cocoa in any recipe that calls for cocoa and it will work fine.

Erythritol, powdered: While erythritol is widely used as a sugar replacer, we don't recommend it for our recipes because it has a lower melting point than the suggested substitutes and, thus, causes too much spread. However, it also comes in a powdered form that is appropriate for use as a dusting or garnishing ingredient. Powdered erythritol is sold under a few brand names that are of equal quality, and is mainly available through mail order (see the Resources section for details). Some natural foods markets may also carry it. When you order it just be sure that you are ordering the powdered version, not the granules. The granules do not work well as a garnish.

Fresh fruit and vegetables: If you're very sensitive to sugar, fruit and even some vegetables may be an issue. There are plenty of recipes in this book that don't include fruits and vegetables, and you may want to focus on those. However, we typically call for these ingredients in moderate amounts, and we've formulated the recipes to balance out their sugars. We recommend that you give some of these recipes a try and start with just a very small portion so you can see how they work for you. And if you don't have issues with the sugars in whole fruits, then feel free to increase the amount. We've generally provided guidance on how much you can add without adversely affecting the final product.

Raisins and dried fruit: Dried fruits are even sweeter than their fresh counterparts, so we don't call for them often. But again, when we do, the amounts are moderate and the overall glycemic load of the final product is carefully balanced, so you may be able to enjoy these treats in moderation. And if you aren't sensitive to the sugars in dried fruit, you can increase the amount if you like.

Salt: We generally prefer sea salt or kosher salt because they are pure and have a clean flavor. For baking, we use regular-grind sea salt and the smaller grind of kosher salt, and this is what we mean when we say just plain "salt" in ingredient lists. Don't substitute coarser forms of salt; they weigh less, spoon for spoon, and that difference can affect the flavor of the final product. If you have only coarse salt, increase the amount by about 25 percent. Also, note that because the amount of salt in these recipes is so low, you can also use iodized table salt if you like.

Spray oil: There are so many vegetable oil sprays on the market, such as Pam, Spectrum, and Smart Balance. Spray oil is used primarily to prevent sticking, so any type will do except those that contain flour (the label will usually say "For Baking," but check the ingredients list to be certain). However, we recommend butter-flavored sprays because of how nicely they enhance the flavor of nut flour. Regardless of what variety you choose, be sure to have some on hand, because we call for it in almost every recipe!

Sugar-free maple-flavored syrup: If sugar isn't an issue for you, then we highly recommend that you use pure maple syrup. But since you're reading this book, we bet that you or someone you love is sensitive to sugar. Fortunately, there are some serviceable sugar-free maple-flavored syrups on the market. We recommend Maple Grove Farms Sugar-Free Maple-Flavored Syrup and Vermont Sugar-Free Syrup. Please note that Maple Grove Farms brand is a company that also makes excellent pure maple syrup, but they make both of these two sugar-free brands, which is probably why their products taste better to us than any of the other sugar-free brands—they know real maple syrup. The sugar-free version, labeled Vermont Sugar-Free Syrup, contains only 5 grams of carbs per ¼ cup serving. The Maple Grove Farms Sugar-Free Maple-Flavored Syrup contains 12 carbs per serving (by way of comparison, there are 53 net carbs in an equal amount of pure maple syrup). Both are labeled "sugar-free," but the *Vermont* Sugar-Free version has the least amount of carbs, so purchase that one if carbs are a concern. If you can't find this brand, you can find other sugar-free maple-flavored syrups in most grocery stores alongside the other syrups. Read the labels carefully and opt for the one with the fewest carbs.

Xanthan gum: Gums are often used as gluten replacements because they stabilize and thicken products. Guar gum, derived from guar beans, is one type, but we prefer xanthan gum because it is easier to digest than guar gum, which causes gas in some people. However, if you already use guar gum feel free to continue using it in these recipes. Xanthan gum is derived from the fermentation of glucose or other sugars and is dried into a powder that forms a gum when it is hydrated. There is no glycemic load from the small amount of gum used in these recipes.

THE GLUTEN-FREE, SUGAR-FREE TOOL KIT

For the most part, the tools you'll need to make these recipes are identical to those found in any well-equipped kitchen. However, a few special items will come in handy, and we also have some pointers on a few tools.

Baking pans: You'll need a variety of baking pans for the recipes in this book: rimmed baking sheets (typically 13 by 18 inches), round or rectangular cake pans, loaf pans, mini loaf pans, springform tube pans, Bundt pans, muffin pans, and a few others. But don't feel you have to rush out and buy all of these if you don't already have them. You can buy them along the way, as the need arises. For that matter, you can also use disposable pans at first,

while you're assessing how much baking you're likely to do. Double-layered, insulated pans are also great, as they cook more evenly and protect the bottoms of products such as cookies or scones (you can also double pan these products if you find that they need it). As you begin baking these products you will quickly be able to assess whether you will need to double pan or use insulated pans, depending on how your oven bakes.

Blender: If you don't have a seed grinder or food processor, you can use a blender to make nut and seed flour. Just be sure to follow the instructions on page 13 and don't blend for too long, or you may end up with nut or seed butter.

Bowls: It's handy to have an assortment of stainless steel mixing bowls of various sizes. You can also use glass or ceramic bowls, but they are more vulnerable to chipping or breaking.

Bread knife: The breads and other baked goods in this book are a bit more prone to crumbling than traditional baked goods. A sharp, high-quality serrated knife will go a long way toward ensuring slicing success.

Cookie cutters or biscuit cutters: These are convenient for cutting out the dough for crackers. A 2-inch round cutter is the perfect size for crackers.

Digital kitchen scale: Measuring by weight is always more accurate than using scoops, especially for flours. Using the weight measurements when given will probably yield superior results without the need for adjustments to amounts or cooking times. If you don't have a scale, the volume measurements provided will work fine.

Electric mixer: An electric mixer isn't essential for most of the recipes in this book, but if you have one, it will make easy work of the mixing. Refer to the instructions on page 27 for guidance on using an electric mixer with the recipes in this book.

Food processor: If you don't have a seed grinder, a food processor is your next best bet for doing the job. Use the metal blade attachment and follow the instructions on page 13. A food processor is also handy for grating carrots, cheese, and other ingredients, and for making pesto.

Ice cream scoops: Sure, you're going to want to scoop up some sugar-free ice cream to top your baked treats on special occasions. But you'll also find ice cream scoops helpful, day in, day out, for scooping batter into muffin pans.

Measuring spoons and cups: Of course, you cannot bake without a set of measuring spoons and a set of measuring cups. Better yet, have two sets of each so you can use one set for liquid ingredients and the other for dry ingredients.

Metal spatulas: These come in a variety of styles and are suited to numerous tasks, from flipping pancakes to icing cakes.

Mixing spoons: Most of the doughs and batters in this book are very easy to mix by hand and come together in a matter of minutes. Still, a large sturdy spoon is definitely the best choice.

Muffin liners: Whether you go with paper or foil muffin liners, they will make it so much easier to extract muffins from the pan. They also speed cleanup. What's not to like about that? But, if you don't have any, we offer in the recipe section an alternative method for preparing pans so that the muffins will release easily.

Parchment paper or silicone baking mats: It's always a good idea to line baking pans with parchment paper or a silicone mat. This protects the dough from oxidation and also ensures that your baked goods won't stick.

Pizza cutter: This nifty tool is very useful for crackers and also for . . . well . . . pizzas.

Rolling pin: When you make crackers or piecrusts, a rolling pin is essential for rolling them out evenly and thinly.

Rubber spatulas: We're sure you don't want to waste even one iota of the delicious batters and doughs you'll be making. If you don't already have several rubber spatulas on hand, invest in a few so you always have a clean one, ready to scrape the bowl.

Seed grinder: Of all the tools listed here, this is probably the one you're least likely to have—but it's also one of the most important. Although you can use a food processor or blender to make nut and seed flours, a seed grinder does a superior job of grinding nuts and seeds into flour without overheating them (see page 13 for full instructions). You can also use an electric coffee or spice grinder for this purpose (though coffee grinders sometimes get clogged), and you may discover devices marketed for all of these purposes. Whatever name they go by, these grinders are commonly available at cookware stores or in cookware departments and can be a very economical (and fun) purchase. Denene loves her Cuisinart Nut Seed Grinder (about $55), and Peter feels the same way about his Bosch Seed and Spice Grinder (about $45).

Whisk: We find whisking to be the easiest way to combine both dry and wet ingredients. Of course, you'll want to use a dry whisk when stirring dry ingredients together. And if you have a strong whisk, you can just keep mixing with that when combining wet and dry ingredients.

GLUTEN-FREE, LOW-CARB BAKING METHODS

The bread recipes in this book are essentially quick breads. As mentioned, yeast can't be used to leaven these doughs because there aren't enough carbs available to feed the yeast. In the few recipes where we use yeast, it's purpose is flavoring, not leavening. Although these recipes don't yield the flavors and textures of traditional breads, the final results are tasty and satisfying—and come with the huge bonus of streamlined preparation time. So, the first step is typically preheating the oven and preparing the pans. By the time you finish mixing the dough, the oven should be hot and ready to bake your creations!

The sections below will take you through the most common steps. All are straightforward, but if you have questions, consult our website: www.thejoyofgluten-freesugar-freebaking.com.

Mixing

Most of these recipes are easily mixed by hand. In the few cases where an electric mixer can make a big difference, we specify that in the method but also provide instructions for hand mixing for those who don't have a mixer. As you'll see, we typically call for mixing the dry ingredients first, then mixing the wet ingredients in a larger bowl and stirring in the dry ingredients. In most cases, you could do it the other way around, adding the wet ingredients to the dry, but in some cases it does matter, so we recommend sticking with the instructions as written. One advantage to our method is that you can use the same measuring utensils and even the same whisk for both mixtures if you combine the dry ingredients first. But the bottom line is that these recipes are so forgiving that you can hardly mess them up unless you measure incorrectly.

Mixing by Hand

If you can stir, you can mix these doughs! Most of the recipes call for first putting all of the dry ingredients in the bowl and whisking until well mixed. Next, all of the liquid ingredients are combined in a separate bowl and whisked until thoroughly blended. You'll see that eggs are generally the first wet ingredient listed. If you put them in the bowl first, you can whisk them a bit before adding the remaining liquid ingredients to speed mixing if you like, but this isn't necessary.

Once the liquid ingredients are mixed, simply add the dry ingredients to the wet ingredients and stir with a large, sturdy spoon until evenly combined. Because these recipes are gluten-free, there's no need to develop any gluten, and therefore no need to knead and no fear of overmixing because there's no gluten to toughen up the dough! Mixing takes only as long as required to thoroughly combine all of the ingredients, usually less than 2 minutes. Occasionally we call for mixing the dough for a few minutes to aerate it slightly, which yields a better rise. As in any recipe, it's a good idea to scrape down the sides of the bowl a few times during mixing, to make sure all of the ingredients are evenly incorporated.

Mixing with an Electric Mixer

If you use an electric mixer, the procedure is essentially the same; it just requires less muscle power. Start by whisking the dry ingredients together in a bowl. Next, put all of the liquid ingredients in a separate bowl or the bowl of a stand mixer with the paddle attachment and mix at low speed until thoroughly blended, starting with any eggs if you wish. Then, with the mixer still running at low speed, slowly add the dry ingredients. Once they're added, increase the speed to medium and mix until thoroughly combined. Where longer mixing is required to aerate the mixture, the instructions will specify this. And, as with hand mixing, scrape down the sides of the bowl from time to time to make sure all of the ingredients are evenly incorporated.

Note that in a few recipes we call for beating egg whites or cream until peaks form. This task is arduous by hand, and in these instances an electric mixer is your best bet. Likewise, a few of the mixtures are very stiff, especially those calling for cream cheese. In all of these cases we've written the primary instructions to use an electric mixer, with hand mixing given as an option.

Using Texture as a Guide

Within each recipe, you will see cues for how the dough should look and feel. Here are examples of what we mean:

- **Thick, sticky** dough means that the consistency of the dough will resemble cooked oatmeal or porridge, and it will be sticky. A spatula or wooden spoon will stand straight up when inserted into the center of the mixture. The dough will hold its shape when dropped from a spoon, and is even moldable once transferred to a baking sheet. This description applies to many of the recipes for breads, cookies, hush puppies, and

crackers. In some instances, we will say *very thick and sticky*, which means it's even thicker and almost, but not quite, stiff.

- In these recipes, our description of **stiff** dough is often punctuated with the words "playdough-like," because not only will a spatula or spoon stand straight up when inserted into the center of the dough, but also the dough will hold its shape when formed into scones, biscuits, breadsticks, pretzels, piecrusts, and cookies. It won't stick to your fingers the way a thick batter does, and peels off much like playdough does.

- **Smooth, sticky** dough (which is aerated or made fluffy in some recipes, and also pourable in some instances), such as pizza or focaccia dough, as well as some bread and cake doughs, requires a pan to help it hold its shape. These smooth doughs are often poured or spread into the pans rather than formed into freestanding shapes. When working with these doughs, use wet hands and tools (dipped into some water or rubbed with oil) to keep the dough from sticking to your hands.

- **Loose, pourable** dough, used in our recipes for pancakes and waffles, is slightly thicker than a milkshake and is the loosest of the doughs.

If any of your doughs don't conform to these cues, adjust the liquid or flour amounts accordingly. In most cases, a different consistency means that one of the ingredients was drier than usual, or the ingredients may have been measured out incorrectly.

Shaping

Because these baked goods are generally made in loaf pans, muffin tins, and other such pans, you don't need to learn elaborate shaping techniques, as for traditional breads. In most cases, the dough or batter is simply poured or portioned into pans and then baked. In recipes where shaping is required, here are a few pointers to help ensure success:

- When shaping dough by hand, as when rolling balls of dough for cloverleaf rolls, oiling your hands or spraying them with pan spray, or even dipping them in water, will help prevent sticking.

- Because these doughs tend to be soft and on the sticky side, when manipulating dough on a work surface, it's best to oil the surface or spray it with oil to prevent sticking.

Baking

The temperatures indicated in these recipes are for conventional ovens. If you have a convection oven, reduce the temperature by 25°F or 14°C. If you have an older convection oven with a very strong fan, reduce the temperature by 50°F or about 28°C. Because every oven is different, these adjustments are just approximations. Once you make a few of these recipes, you'll have a better idea of whether you need to adjust the baking temperatures and by how much.

You'll note that we often call for lining bakeware with parchment paper or a silicone mat. Although new baking pans usually have a protective glaze that prevents the metal from reacting with the food, over time and with use, this coating glaze wears off and the metal becomes more exposed. In some instances, the metal may react to acids in the dough, discoloring your baked goods or even imparting a metallic taste. Whenever you can line the pan with a silicone mat, this is your best bet for avoiding these problems—and also has the benefit of releasing baked goods easily. Parchment paper is also an option, but it isn't truly nonstick until the paper heats up, so we generally recommend that you mist the parchment paper with spray oil to ensure an easy release. However, note that some doughs are dry enough that they don't tend to stick, so in these cases we don't call for misting the parchment. All of that said, if you don't have parchment paper or a silicone mat, you can definitely bake directly on the pan; you may just want to oil it more generously. We also give instructions for preparing shaped baking pans such as Bundt pans by generously greasing the pan, freezing it, then coating the interior with nut flour just before it's used.

For baking a single sheet pan, we recommend putting it on a rack positioned in the middle of the oven. For two or more pans, your best bet is probably to bake just one pan at a time. In this case, you'd want to use double-acting baking powder (see page 18) to ensure a good rise on items that go into the oven later. For two pans, another option is to position two racks in the center of the oven with enough space between them to accommodate the pans and allow for some air space above and below.

There are very few ovens that bake evenly, so, as is common for all baked goods, we suggest rotating pans halfway through the baking time (this includes switching racks, too, if baking in two pans) to ensure even baking, and the recipes include this instruction. However, in some instances, you may need to wait until later in the baking process to rotate. An example would be if a cake hasn't set up in the suggested time frame. Use your best judgment. If you find that your oven bakes evenly (which is more likely with a convection oven), then there may be no need to rotate.

Cooling and Storing

Cooling is always an important part of the baking process, mainly because it comes right before eating! But in all seriousness, from a technical standpoint baked goods are still baking when they first come out of the oven. One definition of baking is "the application of heat to a product in an enclosed environment (the oven) for the purpose of driving off moisture." Once removed from the oven, they're no longer enclosed, but the residual heat is still driving off moisture—and intensifying flavors and firming up in the process. This is especially true with these wet, dense batters. Leave the just-baked products uncovered to finish cooling, until they cool for at least as long as prompted in the instructions, or until cool to the touch. Loaf breads may be sliced and eaten after they cool as directed, but are even easier to slice after a thorough cooling in the refrigerator, as directed opposite. Wire racks are best for cooling most baked goods because they allow moisture to evaporate on all sides, including underneath.

Once your baked goods are completely cooled, store them in airtight containers or resealable freezer bags. Because they are made with nut and seed flours, they contain more oils than most traditional baked goods, so put a paper towel in the container or bag to absorb any oil that works its way to the surface. You can store your baked goods at room temperature for a day or so, but we recommend keeping them in the refrigerator or freezer for optimum flavor and freshness. Remember, the primary ingredients are nut and seed flours, and their oils are vulnerable to rancidity.

READY, SET, BAKE!

This chapter of basics has given you all of the information you need to get started. Now all you need is experience, so choose a recipe that appeals to you and give it a try. You can always refer to this chapter if you need to, but once you start making these recipes, you'll undoubtedly find them easier than you'd ever imagined they could be—not to mention extremely delicious. Now you can fill your home with tasty, healthful, guilt-free baked goods. You can enjoy them whenever you want a treat or as an accompaniment to meals, and you can feel great about giving them to your kids, friends, and loved ones. A new era of baking awaits.

Chapter One

BREADS AND ROLLS

The recipes in this chapter will give you a solid foundation in baking gluten-free, sugar-free, low-carb bread. Once you've tried a few of the recipes as written, you can start to branch out by substituting different flours, creating as many bread variations as you can imagine. We'll add new recipes to the website as we develop them, or as you share them (see page 10 for more details on the website).

Although we've divided the recipes into seemingly neat categories of breads and rolls, the truth is, you can use the bread doughs to make rolls and vice versa.

These breads aren't leavened with yeast, as the low-carb content and absence of sugar mean there's little or no food for yeast, so it cannot grow and ferment. In that sense, these are really quick breads, leavened with baking powder, and for that reason, they should be baked as soon as the dough is made. If you miss the yeasty flavor of regular bread, feel free to add a packet of instant or active dry yeast (2¼ teaspoons) to any of these recipes. Dissolve it in 2 tablespoons of warm water; the temperature should be about 95°F (35°C). Add the mixture to the wet ingredients and proceed with mixing as described in the recipe. It's just for flavor, not leavening, and it's totally optional.

Here are some tips and tricks that apply to all of the breads in this chapter:

- Because various brands of nut flour, levels of grind, and types of nuts absorb liquid differently, you may need to adjust these recipes by adding more liquid or nut flour to achieve the batter texture we describe. Keep in mind that most of these batters should be thick but pourable.

- It's best to let the loaves cool completely before slicing them, though you can slice thick slices while still warm. If you like thinner slices, chill the cooled bread first to firm it up.

- As with all products made with nut and seed flour, store these breads in the refrigerator or freezer. If freezing, you can slice the bread and freeze the slices; that way you can take them out of the freezer as you need them without thawing the whole loaf.

- Baking with nut and seed flours results in breads that are rich in natural oils. To maintain freshness, store the bread in a plastic container or resealable bag lined with a paper towel. The paper towel will absorb any oil that seeps out of the loaf and will also help maintain the freshness of the bread longer (the paper towel controls moisture, which could otherwise ruin the loaf).

- When making rolls, you can bake them in a muffin tin to help them hold their shape and height. Or for flatter, more rustic rolls, bake them on a baking sheet. If using a muffin tin, mist the cups with spray oil; if using a baking sheet, line it with parchment paper or a silicone mat. Round rolls may take longer to bake than cloverleaf rolls—perhaps about 10 minutes longer. For best results, use the doneness cues to determine when to remove the rolls from the oven.

Toasting Bread

MAKES 1 LARGE LOAF (10 TO 12 SLICES), OR 4 TO 6 MINI LOAVES

Although this method uses neither yeast nor fermentation, this is a totally satisfying loaf that really comes alive when toasted, developing a wonderful crackly surface. Unlike some gluten-free breads, it isn't dry; rather, it has a moist, creamy mouthfeel that makes you want to keep popping more slices into the toaster. The recipe has a lot of flaxseed meal, which not only adds fiber and healthful omega-3 fatty acids but also contributes to the bread's rich flavor profile. The whole flaxseeds are optional, but adding them will boost those qualities even more. If you find the flaxseed flavor too strong for your liking, replace some of the flaxseed meal with an equal amount of almond flour. You can also replace the sesame seeds or whole flaxseeds with almond flour, but we prefer the crunch factor and flavor the whole seeds lend to the bread.

The liquid stevia is optional as well. We recommend that you use it if you'll be serving the bread slathered with butter or sugar-free jam for breakfast or snacking. If you plan to use it for sandwiches, leave out the liquid stevia. One final note: Because this recipe calls for so many egg whites, we recommend that you purchase liquid egg whites so you don't have a quandary about what to do with all of the yolks. To use liquid egg whites, simply weigh out the amount specified in the recipe.

2 cups (8 oz / 227 g) brown or golden flaxseed meal

2 cups (8 oz / 227 g) pecan flour (see page 12)

1/4 cup (1.15 oz / 32 g) sesame seeds

1/4 cup (1.4 oz / 40 g) whole flaxseeds (optional)

4 teaspoons baking powder

1 teaspoon xanthan gum

1/2 teaspoon salt

1 1/2 cups (12 oz / 340 g) unsweetened soy milk or other milk

8 egg whites (10 oz / 283 g)

1/4 to 1/2 teaspoon liquid stevia (optional)

Preheat the oven to 375°F (191°C). Line the bottom of a 4½ by 8-inch loaf pan with parchment paper, then mist the pan with spray oil. (If making mini loaves, forgo the parchment paper and simply coat the pans generously with spray oil.)

In a medium bowl, combine the flaxseed meal, pecan flour, sesame seeds, flaxseeds, baking powder, xanthan gum, and salt and whisk until well mixed. In a large bowl, whisk the milk, egg whites, and liquid stevia together until thoroughly blended. Add the flour mixture and stir vigorously with a large spoon for about 2 minutes to make a thick, sticky, slightly aerated batter (see page 27).   (CONTINUED)

Pour the mixture into the prepared pan or pans, filling them to about ½ inch from the top. For a large loaf, bake for 45 minutes, then rotate and bake for an additional 35 to 45 minutes; for mini loaves, bake for 30 minutes, then rotate and bake for 25 to 30 minutes. The bread is fully cooked when golden brown and springy when pressed in the center.

Transfer to a wire rack and let cool for at least 5 minutes. Before turning out the loaf, run an icing spatula or thin knife around the edges to loosen the bread from the sides. Cool for at least 15 more minutes before slicing. Store the bread in the refrigerator.

Sesame Seed Bread

You can use either brown or golden flaxseed meal in this excellent sandwich bread. Brown flaxseeds will give it a nuttier taste, whereas the flavor of golden flaxseeds is mellower. The toasted sesame seeds add a long-lasting finish to the flavor—thirty minutes after you eat this bread, its flavors are still with you.

1¹/₂ cups (6 oz / 170 g) sesame seed flour

¹/₂ cup (2 oz / 57 g) brown or golden flaxseed meal

2 tablespoons sesame seeds, lightly toasted (see Tip, page 172)

2 teaspoons baking powder

1 teaspoon xanthan gum

¹/₂ teaspoon salt

3 eggs (5.25 oz / 149 g)

¹/₄ cup (2 oz / 57 g) unsweetened soy milk or other milk

¹/₄ teaspoon liquid stevia (optional)

Preheat the oven to 375°F (191°C). Line the bottom of a 4½ by 8-inch loaf pan with parchment paper, then mist the pan with spray oil.

In a medium bowl, combine the sesame seed flour, flaxseed meal, sesame seeds, baking powder, xanthan gum, and salt and whisk until well mixed. In a large bowl, whisk the eggs, milk, and liquid stevia together until thoroughly blended. Add the flour mixture and stir with a large spoon for 1 to 2 minutes to make a thick, sticky batter (see page 27).

Pour the mixture into the prepared pan. Bake for 25 minutes, then rotate and bake for an additional 25 to 30 minutes, until golden brown and springy when pressed in the center and a toothpick inserted into the middle of the loaf comes out clean.

Let the bread cool in the pan for at least 5 minutes before turning out the loaf. Let cool on a wire rack for at least 15 minutes before slicing and serving.

VARIATION

Triple-Sesame Bread: For more crunch and a stronger sesame flavor, coat the top of the loaf with about ¼ cup (1 oz / 28 g) of raw sesame seeds just prior to baking.

"Stout" Bread

MAKES 1 LOAF (10 TO 12 SLICES)

This hearty bread, which toasts up beautifully, is made with garbanzo bean flour (ground chickpeas) and is almost a meal in itself. As the name says, it's stout. That doesn't refer to beer; it's a reference to the thick, solid texture of the bread. It has a wonderfully crunchy crust and a deep, old-world flavor with a slightly peppery finish, making it a good companion for all types of soups and stews.

This is a recipe that is easier to make with an electric mixer because the batter is very stiff, though you can make it by hand if necessary.

2 cups (8 oz / 227 g) garbanzo bean flour (see Tip)

1 cup (4 oz / 113 g) golden flaxseed meal

1/2 cup (2.75 oz / 78 g) whole golden or brown flaxseeds

1/4 cup Splenda or Stevia Extract in the Raw, or 2 tablespoons New Roots Stevia Sugar

4 teaspoons baking powder

1 teaspoon xanthan gum

1/2 teaspoon salt

1/2 teaspoon finely ground black pepper (optional)

4 eggs (7 oz / 198 g)

1 cup (8 oz / 227 g) unsweetened soy milk or other milk

1 cup (8 oz / 227 g) water

1/2 cup (4 oz / 113 g) salted butter or margarine, melted

Tip: Working with Garbanzo Bean Flour

Although a variety of legume flours are available, we believe that garbanzo bean flour is one of the few that diabetics can generally use without risking a spike in blood sugar. However, some diabetics do experience glycemic spikes even with garbanzo bean flour, so monitor your blood sugar closely to determine whether it works for you.

Bob's Red Mill and a few other companies make garbanzo bean flour, so you can purchase it if you like. If it isn't available locally, you can buy it online. Or, as with nut and seed flours, you can make it at home. Because the dried beans are so hard, you'll need to work in smaller batches, and it does take a while to grind them into a fine flour. The more finely you grind them, the softer the final loaf.

Preheat the oven to 375°F (191°C). Line a 4½ by 8-inch loaf pan with parchment paper, then mist the pan with spray oil.

In a medium bowl, combine the garbanzo bean flour, flaxseed meal, whole flaxseeds, sweetener, baking powder, xanthan gum, salt, and pepper. Whisk until well mixed.

In a large bowl or the bowl of an electric mixer, combine the eggs, milk, water, and butter and whisk or mix with the paddle attachment at medium-low speed until thoroughly blended. Add the flour mixture and stir vigorously with a large spoon or mix at medium speed for 2 minutes. Scrape down the sides of the bowl, then stir even more vigorously by hand or mix at medium-high speed for 3 minutes. The extended mixing helps aerate this very thick, sticky batter (see page 27).

Pour or spoon the mixture into the prepared pan. Bake for 40 minutes, then rotate and bake for about 40 more minutes, until golden brown and springy when pressed in the center and a toothpick inserted into the middle of the loaf comes out clean.

Let the bread cool in the pan for at least 5 minutes before turning out the loaf. Let cool on a wire rack for at least 15 minutes before slicing and serving.

Garbanzo-Onion Bread

MAKES 1 LOAF (10 TO 12 SLICES)

This rich and savory bread is made with garbanzo bean (chickpea) flour and, for a unique twist, chicken broth or vegetable broth, creating a complex depth of flavor. For optimum results, we recommend that you use fresh, homemade broth, but store-bought broth will also work.

We strongly recommend using an electric mixer with this recipe, as garbanzo bean flour makes a very thick, stiff batter that may be difficult to mix by hand.

2 cups (8 oz / 227 g) garbanzo bean flour (see Tip, page 38)

1 cup (4 oz / 113 g) almond flour

1/4 cup Splenda or Stevia Extract in the Raw, or 2 tablespoons New Roots Stevia Sugar

4 teaspoons baking powder

1 teaspoon xanthan gum

1/2 teaspoon salt

4 eggs (7 oz / 198 g)

1 cup (8 oz / 227 g) low-sodium chicken broth or vegetable broth

1 cup (8 oz / 227 g) water

1/2 cup (4 oz / 113 g) salted butter or margarine, melted

1/2 cup (3.25 oz / 92 g) chopped fresh onion

Preheat the oven to 375°F (191°C). Line the bottom of a 4½ by 8-inch loaf pan with parchment paper, then mist the pan with spray oil.

In a medium bowl, combine the garbanzo bean flour, almond flour, sweetener, baking powder, xanthan gum, and salt and whisk until well mixed. In a large bowl, whisk the eggs, broth, water, and butter together until thoroughly blended. Stir in the onion. Add the flour mixture and stir with the paddle attachment of a stand mixer or a large spoon for 1 to 2 minutes to make a very thick, sticky batter (see page 27).

Pour or spoon the mixture into the prepared pan. Bake for 40 minutes, then rotate and bake for about 40 more minutes, until golden brown and springy when pressed in the center and a toothpick inserted into the middle of the loaf comes out clean.

Let the bread cool in the pan for at least 5 minutes before turning out the loaf. Let cool on a wire rack for at least 15 minutes before slicing and serving.

Onion and Poppy Seed Bread

MAKES 1 LOAF (10 TO 12 SLICES)

Savory and full of onion flavor, this fun bread complements any soup and is also great with fish or chicken dishes.

1¹/₂ cups (6 oz / 170 g) golden flaxseed meal

1¹/₂ cups (6 oz / 170 g) sesame seed flour

¹/₄ cup Splenda or Stevia Extract in the Raw, or 2 tablespoons New Roots Stevia Sugar

4 teaspoons baking powder

2 teaspoons poppy seeds

1 teaspoon xanthan gum

1 teaspoon salt

4 eggs (7 oz / 198 g)

1 cup (8 oz / 227 g) unsweetened soy milk or other milk

¹/₂ cup (4 oz / 113 g) salted butter or margarine, melted

¹/₂ cup (3.25 oz / 92 g) chopped fresh onion

Preheat the oven to 375°F (191°C). Line the bottom of a 4½ by 8-inch loaf pan with parchment paper, then mist the pan with spray oil.

In a medium bowl, combine the flaxseed meal, sesame seed flour, sweetener, baking powder, poppy seeds, xanthan gum, and salt. Whisk until well mixed. In a large bowl, whisk the eggs, milk, and butter together until thoroughly blended. Stir in the onion. Add the flour mixture and stir with a large spoon for 1 to 2 minutes to make a thick, sticky batter (see page 27).

Pour the mixture into the prepared pan. Bake for 40 minutes, then rotate and bake for about 40 more minutes, until golden brown and springy when pressed in the center and a toothpick inserted into the middle of the loaf comes out clean.

Let the bread cool in the pan for at least 5 minutes before turning out the loaf. Let cool on a wire rack for at least 15 minutes before slicing and serving.

VARIATIONS

Extra-Onion Bread: If you love the flavor of onions, you can double the amount of onion.

Onion, Poppy Seed, and Sesame Seed Bread: For another layer of flavor, add ¼ cup (1 oz / 28 g) of toasted sesame seeds (see Tip, page 172), adding them with the dry ingredients or simply sprinkling the seeds over the top of the loaf just before baking.

Any Nut Bread

MAKES 1 LOAF (10 TO 12 SLICES)

This is an excellent and versatile nut bread that can be made with any type of nut—the batter is a blank canvas, so feel free to use your favorite nut (pistachio, walnut, peanut, macadamia, hazelnut, cashew, and more are all fair game). This version uses chopped pecans, but any nut will work, which means this recipe can really be made in multiple variations. Lightly toasting the nuts is optional, but it will intensify their flavor. If you'll be using your loaf for sandwiches or to accompany savory dishes, use the lesser amount of sweetener. Or add the full amount of sweetener and enjoy the loaf as a quick bread, served warm or toasted and topped with sugar-free jam.

3 cups (12 oz / 340 g) almond flour

$^3/_4$ cup pecans or your favorite nuts, raw or toasted (see Tip, page 172), chopped into small and medium-size bits

$^1/_4$ to 1 cup Splenda or Stevia Extract in the Raw, or 2 tablespoons to $^1/_2$ cup New Roots Stevia Sugar, depending on desired sweetness

4 teaspoons baking powder

1 teaspoon xanthan gum

$^1/_2$ teaspoon salt

4 eggs (7 oz / 198 g)

1 cup (8 oz / 227 g) unsweetened soy milk or other milk

$^1/_4$ cup (2 oz / 57 g) salted butter or margarine, melted

Preheat the oven to 375°F (191°C). Line the bottom of a 4½ by 8-inch loaf pan with parchment paper, then mist the pan with spray oil.

In a medium bowl, combine the almond flour, pecans, sweetener, baking powder, xanthan gum, and salt and whisk until well mixed.

In a large bowl or the bowl of an electric mixer, combine the eggs, milk, and butter and whisk or mix with the paddle attachment at medium-low speed until thoroughly blended. Add the flour mixture and stir vigorously with a large spoon or mix at medium speed for 1 to 2 minutes. Scrape down the sides of the bowl, then stir even more vigorously by hand or mix at medium-high speed for 1 to 2 minutes to make a thick, sticky, somewhat aerated batter (see page 27).

Pour the mixture into the prepared pan. Bake for 35 minutes, then rotate and bake for about 35 more minutes, until golden brown and springy when pressed in the center and a toothpick inserted into the middle of the loaf comes out clean.

Let the bread cool in the pan for at least 5 minutes before turning out the loaf. Let cool on a wire rack for at least 15 minutes before slicing and serving.

Hazelnut Bread

MAKES 1 LOAF (10 TO 12 SLICES)

The pleasant hazelnut flavor of this bread makes it a unique and wonderful option for sandwiches, and the nutty flavor works well with just about any type of sandwich fixings.

3 cups (12 oz / 340 g) hazelnut flour

1/2 cup (2 oz / 57 g) coconut flour (see Tip, page 14)

1/4 cup Splenda or Stevia Extract in the Raw, or 2 tablespoons New Roots Stevia Sugar

4 teaspoons baking powder

1 teaspoon xanthan gum

1/2 teaspoon salt

1/4 teaspoon ground ginger

4 eggs (7 oz / 198 g)

3/4 cup (6 oz / 170 g) water

1/2 cup (4 oz / 113 g) unsweetened soy milk or other milk

1/2 cup (4 oz / 113 g) salted butter or margarine, melted

Preheat the oven to 375°F (191°C). Line the bottom of a 4½ by 8-inch loaf pan with parchment paper, then mist the pan with spray oil.

In a medium bowl, combine the hazelnut flour, coconut flour, sweetener, baking powder, xanthan gum, salt, and ginger, and whisk until well mixed. In a large bowl, whisk the eggs, water, milk, and butter together until thoroughly blended. Add the flour mixture and stir with a large spoon for 1 to 2 minutes to make a thick, sticky batter (see page 27).

Pour the mixture into the prepared pan. Bake for 40 minutes, then rotate and bake for about 40 more minutes, until golden brown and springy when pressed in the center and a toothpick inserted into the middle of the loaf comes out clean.

Let the bread cool in the pan for about 5 minutes before turning out the loaf. Let cool on a wire rack for at least 15 minutes before slicing and serving.

VARIATION

Hazelnut-Flaxseed Bread: Add ¼ cup (1 oz / 28 g) of whole flaxseeds, lightly toasted (see Tip, page 172), when mixing the dry ingredients.

Basic Brown Bread

MAKES 1 LOAF (10 TO 12 SLICES)

Full of flaxseeds and enhanced by hazelnut flour, this excellent bread has a mild taste that works well with nearly any kind of sandwich filling. It also toasts up nicely and makes excellent croutons (see page 56). We recommend using an electric mixer for this one, as the final texture is better if the batter is whipped at high speed to aerate it. By the way, if you use golden flaxseed meal instead of brown flaxseed meal, the loaf will have a more golden color, in which case you should feel free to call it Golden Bread! Either way, it is equally delicious and nutritious. To use this as a sandwich loaf, let the loaf sit at room temperature overnight. This extended cooling and tempering period will help bolster the bread's structure.

2 cups (8 oz / 227 g) brown or golden flaxseed meal

1 cup (4 oz / 113 g) hazelnut flour

1/4 cup Splenda or Stevia Extract in the Raw, or 2 tablespoons New Roots Stevia Sugar

4 teaspoons baking powder

1 teaspoon xanthan gum

1/2 teaspoon salt

4 eggs (7 oz / 198 g)

1 cup (8 oz / 227 g) unsweetened soy milk or other milk

1/4 cup (2 oz / 57 g) water

1/4 cup (2 oz / 57 g) salted butter or margarine, melted

Preheat the oven to 375°F (191°C). Line the bottom of a 4½ by 8-inch loaf pan with parchment paper, then mist the pan with spray oil.

In a medium bowl, combine the flaxseed meal, hazelnut flour, sweetener, baking powder, xanthan gum, and salt. Whisk until well mixed.

In a large bowl or the bowl of an electric mixer, combine the eggs, milk, water, and butter and whisk or mix with the paddle attachment at medium-low speed until thoroughly blended. Add the flour mixture and stir vigorously with a large spoon or mix at medium speed for 2 minutes. Scrape down the sides of the bowl, then stir even more vigorously by hand or mix at medium-high speed for 2 minutes to aerate the batter. It should be smooth, sticky, and pourable (see page 27).

Pour the mixture into the prepared pan. Bake for 35 minutes, then rotate and bake for about 35 more minutes, until golden brown and springy when pressed in the center and a toothpick inserted into the middle of the loaf comes out clean. (CONTINUED)

BASIC BROWN BREAD, *continued*

Let the bread cool in the pan for at least 10 minutes before turning out the loaf. Let cool on a wire rack for at least 30 minutes before slicing and serving.

VARIATION

Seeded Brown Bread: If you want some crunch in the bread, add ¼ to ½ cup (60 to 120 ml) whole flaxseeds or sesame seeds (or a combination of the two) when mixing the dry ingredients.

Rosemary Bread

MAKES 1 LOAF (10 TO 12 SLICES)

With its wonderful earthy flavor and deeply aromatic rosemary, this bread is an excellent choice for sandwiches. The high percentage of flaxseed meal is part of its uniqueness, making the bread very filling and satisfying, but feel free to play with the balance of flours if you like. However, we find that the high proportion of flaxseeds works well in this recipe and yields a bread that's delicious.

2 cups (8 oz / 227 g) brown or golden flaxseed meal

1 cup (4 oz / 113 g) almond flour

2 teaspoons minced fresh rosemary

2 teaspoons baking powder

1 teaspoon xanthan gum

1 teaspoon salt

4 eggs (7 oz / 198 g)

1 cup (8 oz / 227 g) unsweetened soy milk or other milk

1/2 cup (4 oz / 113 g) salted butter or margarine, melted

Preheat the oven to 375°F (191°C). Line a 4½ by 8-inch loaf pan with parchment paper, then mist the pan with spray oil.

In a medium bowl, combine the flaxseed meal, almond flour, rosemary, baking powder, xanthan gum, and salt and whisk until well mixed. In a large bowl, whisk the eggs, milk, and butter together until thoroughly blended. Add the flour mixture and stir with a large spoon for 1 to 2 minutes to make a smooth, sticky, and pourable batter (see page 27).

Pour the mixture into the prepared pan. Bake for 35 minutes, then rotate and bake for about 35 more minutes, until golden brown and springy when pressed in the center and a toothpick inserted into the middle of the loaf comes out clean.

Let the bread cool in the pan for at least 10 minutes before turning out the loaf. Let cool on a wire rack for at least 30 minutes before slicing and serving.

VARIATION

Seeded Rosemary Bread: For more texture and crunch, add ¼ cup (1 oz / 28 g) of whole flaxseeds, chia seeds, or hemp seeds when mixing the dry ingredients.

Italian Herb Bread

MAKES 1 LOAF (10 TO 12 SLICES)

The combination of herbs in this savory loaf is just one possibility among many. Feel free to substitute your favorite herbs for those we suggest. You could also use a blend, such as herbes de Provence, which contains many of the herbs listed here, plus lavender. Whatever herbs you choose, use a light hand—even small quantities of some herbs pack a punch, and too much can easily overwhelm the subtle flavors of the nut and seed flours.

2 cups (8 oz / 227 g) almond flour

1 cup (4 oz / 113 g) brown or golden flaxseed meal

2 teaspoons baking powder

1 teaspoon xanthan gum

1 teaspoon salt

1/2 teaspoon dried basil, or 1 tablespoon minced fresh basil

1/2 teaspoon crushed red pepper flakes, ground black pepper, or a combination

1/2 teaspoon dried rosemary or minced fresh rosemary

1/2 teaspoon dried parsley, or 1 tablespoon minced fresh Italian parsley

1/4 teaspoon dried thyme, or 1 teaspoon minced fresh thyme

1/8 teaspoon dried oregano, or 1/2 teaspoon minced fresh oregano

4 eggs (7 oz / 198 g)

1 cup (8 oz / 227 g) unsweetened soy milk or other milk

1/2 cup (4 oz / 113 g) salted butter or margarine, melted

Preheat the oven to 375°F (191°C). Line a 4½ by 8-inch loaf pan with parchment paper, then mist the pan with spray oil.

In a medium bowl, combine the almond flour, flaxseed meal, baking powder, xanthan gum, salt, basil, red pepper flakes, rosemary, parsley, thyme, and oregano and whisk until well mixed. In a large bowl, whisk the eggs, milk, and butter together until thoroughly blended. Add the flour mixture and stir with a large spoon for 1 to 2 minutes to make a smooth, sticky, and pourable batter (see page 27).

Pour the mixture into the prepared pan. Bake for 35 minutes, then rotate and bake for about 35 more minutes, until golden brown and springy when pressed in the center and a toothpick inserted into the middle of the loaf comes out clean.

Let the bread cool in the pan for at least 10 minutes before turning out the loaf. Let cool on a wire rack for at least 30 minutes before slicing and serving.

VARIATION

Cheese and Herb Bread: Add ½ cup (about 2 oz / 57 g) of any grated cheese when mixing the dry ingredients. Alternatively, sprinkle the cheese over the top of the bread about 4 minutes before it's finished baking, to make a cheese crust. Or for double cheesy goodness, do both!

Simple Cloverleaf Rolls

MAKES 8 ROLLS

Here's an all-purpose, anytime dinner roll, baked in a muffin tin to prevent the dough from spreading or flattening out. One innovation in this recipe is using flour made from toasted sesame seeds, which really boosts the flavor of the rolls. (See page 172 for our tips on toasting sesame seeds.) Just one caution: Before you grind the toasted sesame seeds to make the flour, be sure to let them cool completely; otherwise, you'll end up making sesame butter.

2¹/₂ cups (10 oz / 283 g) almond flour

¹/₂ cup (2 oz / 57 g) toasted sesame seed flour (see headnote)

2 tablespoons Splenda or Stevia Extract in the Raw, or 1 tablespoon New Roots Stevia Sugar

¹/₂ teaspoon baking powder

¹/₂ teaspoon xanthan gum

¹/₂ teaspoon salt

2 eggs (3.5 oz / 99 g)

¹/₄ cup (2 oz / 57 g) salted butter or margarine, melted

Preheat the oven to 350°F (177°C). Mist 8 muffin cups with spray oil.

In a medium bowl, combine the almond flour, sesame seed flour, sweetener, baking powder, xanthan gum, and salt and whisk until well mixed. In a large bowl, whisk the eggs and butter together until thoroughly blended. Add the flour mixture and stir with a large spoon for 1 to 2 minutes to make a very thick, sticky batter (see page 27).

Mist a work surface with spray oil and transfer the dough to the oiled spot. Divide the dough into 8 equal portions. To make each roll, divide one of the pieces into 3 equal portions, then form each into a ball. (You may want to oil your hands to prevent sticking.) Put the 3 dough balls in a muffin cup, arranging them in a triangle. Repeat with all of the remaining dough pieces.

Bake the rolls for 15 minutes, then rotate and bake for about 15 more minutes, until golden brown and springy when pressed.

Let the rolls cool in the pan for 5 minutes, then serve while still warm.

VARIATIONS

Silver Dollar Rolls: Mix the dough as directed, but instead of dividing the 8 pieces of dough into 3 equal portions, leave them whole and form them into rounds. Put them on a baking sheet lined with parchment paper or a silicone mat, then brush the tops with an egg wash made by whisking 1 egg with 2 tablespoons of water. If you like, you can use a knife to cut an X into the top of each roll, about ¼ inch deep. Bake as directed above.

Almond, Sesame, or Poppy Seed Cloverleaf Rolls: Just before baking the rolls, sprinkle sesame seeds, toasted almond slivers, or poppy seeds over the top.

Parsley Cloverleaf Rolls: For a splash of color contrast, add ½ teaspoon of dried parsley when mixing the dry ingredients.

Italian Cloverleaf Rolls

MAKES 8 ROLLS

These rolls are Italian by virtue of the blend of herbs, but the basic, unseasoned dough is an excellent all-purpose basis for any number of roll variations. The predominance of sesame seed flour, which is unusual among our dough recipes, gives these rolls a long-lasting flavor. As always, feel free to play with the varieties and proportions of flour. In this case, you might try using flours made with other seeds, such as sunflower and pumpkin seeds. To make round rolls, follow the instructions for the Silver Dollar Rolls variation on page 51, using the egg wash.

2 cups (8 oz / 227 g) sesame seed flour

1 cup (4 oz / 113 g) almond flour

2 tablespoons Splenda or Stevia Extract in the Raw, or 1 tablespoon New Roots Stevia Sugar

1 teaspoon baking powder

1 teaspoon salt

1/2 teaspoon xanthan gum

1/2 teaspoon dried rosemary, ground in a spice grinder until almost powdery, or fresh rosemary, minced

1/2 teaspoon dried basil

1/4 teaspoon dried thyme

1/8 teaspoon dried oregano

2 eggs (3.5 oz / 99 g)

1/4 cup (2 oz / 57 g) salted butter or margarine, melted

Preheat the oven to 350°F (177°C). Mist 8 muffin cups with spray oil.

In a medium bowl, combine the sesame seed flour, almond flour, sweetener, baking powder, salt, xanthan gum, rosemary, basil, thyme, and oregano and whisk until well mixed. In a large bowl, whisk the eggs and butter together until thoroughly blended. Add the flour mixture and stir with a large spoon for 1 to 2 minutes to make a very thick, sticky batter (see page 27).

Mist a work surface with spray oil and transfer the dough to the oiled spot. Divide the dough into 8 equal portions. To make each roll, divide one of the pieces into 3 equal portions, then form each into a ball. (You may want to oil your hands to prevent sticking.) Put the 3 dough balls in a muffin cup, arranging them in a triangle.

Bake the rolls for 10 minutes, then rotate and bake for about 10 more minutes, until lightly browned and firm to the touch.

Let the rolls cool in the pan for 5 minutes, then turn them out onto a wire rack and serve while still warm.

VARIATION

Herbed Cheese Rolls: Add ¼ cup (about 1 oz / 28 g) of grated cheese when mixing the dry ingredients. Alternatively, sprinkle the cheese over the top of the rolls about 3 minutes before they're finished baking.

Cajun Dinner Rolls

MAKES 8 ROLLS

These spicy rolls are perfect to serve with stews, chowders, and gumbos. You can make them even spicier by increasing the amount of cayenne or adding crushed red pepper flakes. To make round rolls, follow the instructions for the Silver Dollar Rolls variation on page 51, using the egg wash if you like.

2 cups (8 oz / 227 g) almond flour

1 cup (4 oz / 113 g) golden flaxseed meal

2 tablespoons Splenda or Stevia Extract in the Raw, or 1 tablespoon New Roots Stevia Sugar

1 teaspoon baking powder

1 teaspoon salt

1/2 teaspoon xanthan gum

1 teaspoon cayenne pepper

1 teaspoon dried parsley

1/2 teaspoon garlic powder or granulated garlic, or 1 teaspoon pressed or minced fresh garlic

1/2 teaspoon onion powder, or 1 tablespoon dried onion flakes, or 1/4 cup (1.65 oz / 47 g) chopped fresh onion

3 eggs (5.25 oz / 149 g)

1/4 cup (2 oz / 57 g) salted butter or margarine, melted

Preheat the oven to 350°F (177°C). Mist 8 muffin cups with spray oil.

In a medium bowl, combine the almond flour, flaxseed meal, sweetener, baking powder, salt, xanthan gum, cayenne, parsley, garlic powder, and onion powder and whisk until well mixed. In a large bowl, whisk the eggs and butter together until thoroughly blended. Add the flour mixture and stir with a large spoon for 1 to 2 minutes to make a very thick, sticky batter (see page 27).

Mist a work surface with spray oil and transfer the dough to the oiled spot. Divide the dough into 8 equal portions. To make each roll, divide one of the pieces into 3 equal portions, then form each into a ball. (You may want to oil your hands to prevent sticking.) Put the 3 dough balls in a muffin cup, arranging them in a triangle.

Bake the rolls for 15 minutes, then rotate and bake for about 15 more minutes, until golden brown and springy when pressed.

Let the rolls cool in the pan for 5 minutes, then turn them out onto a wire rack and serve while still warm.

VARIATION

Cajun Cheese Rolls: Add 1/4 cup (1 oz / 28 g) of grated Cheddar, mozzarella, or Monterey Jack cheese when mixing the dry ingredients. Alternatively, you can sprinkle the cheese over the top of the rolls about 3 minutes before they're finished baking.

Onion Dinner Rolls

MAKES 8 ROLLS

In addition to lending great flavor to breads and rolls, onions provide wonderful moistness and crunch. This recipe uses a higher proportion of sesame seed flour than most. That, along with the onion, gives these rolls a rich and long-lasting flavor, while the parsley adds a beautiful color contrast. To make round rolls, follow the instructions for the Silver Dollar Rolls variation on page 51, using the egg wash.

2 cups (8 oz / 227 g) sesame seed flour

1 cup (4 oz / 113 g) almond flour

2 tablespoons Splenda or Stevia Extract in the Raw, or 1 tablespoon New Roots Stevia Sugar

1 teaspoon baking powder

1 teaspoon salt

1/2 teaspoon xanthan gum

1 1/2 teaspoons onion powder

1/2 teaspoon dried parsley, or 1 tablespoon minced fresh parsley

2 eggs (3.5 oz / 99 g)

1/4 cup (2 oz / 57 g) salted butter or margarine, melted

1/4 cup (1.65 oz / 47 g) finely chopped fresh onion

Preheat the oven to 350°F (177°C). Mist 8 muffin cups with spray oil.

In a medium bowl, combine the sesame seed flour, almond flour, sweetener, baking powder, salt, xanthan gum, onion powder, and parsley and whisk until well mixed. In a large bowl, whisk the eggs and butter together until thoroughly blended. Stir in the onion. Add the flour mixture and stir with a large spoon for 1 to 2 minutes to make a very thick, sticky batter (see page 27).

Mist a work surface with spray oil and transfer the dough to the oiled spot. Divide the dough into 8 equal portions. To make each roll, divide one of the pieces into 3 equal portions, then form each into a ball. (You may want to oil your hands to prevent sticking.) Put the 3 dough balls in a muffin cup, arranging them in a triangle.

Bake the rolls for 10 minutes, then rotate and bake for about 10 more minutes, until golden brown and springy when pressed.

Let the rolls cool in the pan for 5 minutes, then turn them out onto a wire rack and serve while still warm.

VARIATION

Onion Croutons: Leftover onion rolls make great croutons. Just cut the rolls into small cubes and spread them on a rimmed baking sheet. Bake at 250°F (121°C) for 25 to 35 minutes, until dry and crisp, stirring every 10 minutes so the croutons will be crunchy.

Hot Cross Buns

MAKES 6 LARGE OR 12 SMALL BUNS

Hot cross buns, traditionally served on Palm Sunday and Good Friday in England, are now enjoyed year-round throughout the world. To broaden their audience even further, here's our gluten-free, sugar-free version. These slightly sweet, slightly spicy "muffin-style" rolls make a wonderful after-dinner treat or breakfast bun. They are delicious served warm, with honey-flavored butter or sugar-free maple-flavored syrup.

2 cups (8 oz / 227 g) almond flour

1 cup (4 oz / 113 g) coconut flour (see Tip, page 14)

1/2 cup Splenda or Stevia Extract in the Raw, or 1/4 cup New Roots Stevia Sugar

1 teaspoon baking powder

1 teaspoon salt

1 teaspoon ground allspice

1/4 teaspoon ground cloves, ground ginger, or a combination (optional)

4 eggs (7 oz / 198 g)

1/2 cup (4 oz / 113 g) salted butter or margarine, melted

2 teaspoons vanilla extract

2 1/4 teaspoons (1 package) instant or active dry yeast

2 tablespoons warm water (about 95°F, or 35°C)

Glaze

1 cup Splenda, Stevia Extract in the Raw, Truvia, or ZSweet, or 1/4 cup New Roots Stevia Sugar

2 teaspoons unsweetened soy milk or other milk, plus more as needed

1/2 teaspoon vanilla, lemon, or orange extract

Preheat the oven to 340°F (171°C). For 6 large buns, mist 6 muffin cups with spray oil; for 12 small buns, mist 12 muffin cups with spray oil.

In a medium bowl, combine the almond flour, coconut flour, sweetener, baking powder, salt, allspice, and cloves and whisk until well mixed. In a large bowl, whisk the eggs, butter, and vanilla together until thoroughly blended. In a small bowl, stir the yeast and water together until the yeast dissolves, then stir the mixture into the eggs (no need to wait for the yeast to bubble, because it's only for flavor, not leavening).

Add the flour mixture to the egg mixture and stir with a large spoon for 1 to 2 minutes to make a very thick, sticky batter (see page 27).

Mist a work surface with spray oil and transfer the dough to the oiled spot. Divide the dough into 6 equal portions (for large buns) or 12 equal portions (for small buns). Gently form each piece of dough into a ball (you may want to oil your hands to prevent sticking). Place each ball in a prepared muffin cup. Use a small, sharp knife to cut an X into the top of each bun, about 1/4 inch deep. (See page 50 for an example.) (CONTINUED)

Bake for 15 minutes, then rotate and bake for 10 to 15 minutes, until golden brown and springy when pressed. If making 12 rolls instead of 6, cut the baking time approximately in half, or until golden brown and springy when pressed.

Let the rolls cool in the pan for about 3 minutes, then turn them out onto a wire rack and let cool for about 20 minutes, until just warm to the touch.

Meanwhile, make the glaze. In a small bowl, whisk all of the ingredients together until thoroughly blended and the mixture has a thick, syrupy, ribbonlike consistency. Drizzle the glaze into the cross or over the entire top of the buns by letting it ribbon off the end of a fork or spoon. Alternatively, you can put the glaze in a piping bag or a small plastic sandwich bag with one corner snipped off and pipe it onto the buns.

Hush Puppies

MAKES 30 HUSH PUPPIES

Hush puppies are savory Southern dumplings made by deep-frying small portions of cornmeal dough. This version replaces the typical cornmeal and wheat flour with flaxseed meal and sesame seed flour for a sugar-free, gluten free treat. They are a terrific accompaniment to any fish or chicken dish, and leftovers make a great snack; just reheat them in a hot oven for a few minutes to bring back the crispness. To make them, you'll need a deep fryer or a heavy stainless steel pot that's at least 6 inches deep. We call for soybean oil for frying because it's safe to cook with at high temperatures and doesn't boil over easily. When cooking with hot oil, safety is the priority at all times. Lower the hush puppies into the oil carefully, and keep kids and others at a safe distance to avoid burns. Also, be sure to grind the sesame seeds into a fine flour, as any residual whole seeds may pop during frying.

1 cup (4 oz / 113 g) golden flaxseed meal

1 cup (4 oz / 113 g) sesame seed flour

2 teaspoons baking powder

1 teaspoon Splenda or Stevia Extract in the Raw, or 1/2 teaspoon New Roots Stevia Sugar

1 teaspoon salt

1/2 teaspoon dried parsley

3 eggs (5.25 oz / 149 g)

1 tablespoon salted butter or margarine, melted

1/2 to 3/4 cup (3.25 oz / 92 g to 5.25 oz / 149 g) finely chopped fresh onion

Soybean oil, for deep-frying

In a medium bowl, combine the flaxseed meal, sesame seed flour, baking powder, sweetener, salt, and parsley and whisk until well mixed. In a large bowl, whisk the eggs and butter together until thoroughly blended. Stir in the onion. Add the flour mixture and stir with a large spoon for 1 minute to make a smooth batter, then mix vigorously for another minute to aerate the batter; if using an electric mixer, mix at medium-high speed with the paddle attachment for 2 minutes altogether, to make a very thick, sticky batter (see page 27).

Pour soybean oil into the deep fryer or pot to a depth of 2½ to 3 inches. Heat the oil to 340°F (177°C). Keep a candy or frying thermometer in the oil at all times and don't let the temperature exceed 360°F (182°C) or drop below 320°F (160°C). Cover a plate with 2 layers of paper towels or place a paper towel on top of or under a wire rack. (CONTINUED)

Using a standard soup spoon, scoop up 1 spoonful of dough and use your finger to carefully slide it into the hot oil to test the oil temperature and cooking time. Fry this first hush puppy for 2 minutes, then turn it over with a slotted spoon, skimmer, or tongs and fry for about 2 more minutes, until rich golden brown and crispy looking. If the total cooking time is longer, check the temperature of the oil; if it's under 340°F (171°C), increase the heat slightly.

Begin frying additional hush puppies, using the soup spoon to scoop up 1 heaping spoonful of batter for each and adding as many as fit comfortably without crowding them. Most deep fryers will accommodate about 6 to 8 hush puppies. When the hush puppies are rich golden brown and crispy looking, transfer them to the lined plate or wire rack to cool slightly and drain. Repeat this process until all of the dough is fried. Serve the hush puppies while still hot and crisp.

VARIATION

Spicy Hush Puppies: For a zippier flavor, add up to ½ teaspoon of ground black pepper when mixing the dry ingredients.

Chapter Two

PIZZAS AND FOCACCIAS

Everyone loves pizza, so mastering the recipes in this chapter is a must! For us, pizza, and its northern Italian cousin focaccia, is about the crust first and the toppings second. This chapter includes three recipes for pizza dough, followed by a section with some topping suggestions, and then a number of variations on focaccia. Use them to get started, then explore and create your own variations. Let us know what you come up with via our website, www.thejoyofgluten-freesugar-freebaking.com. We'll try your variations and post some of the success stories on the website.

Here are a few tips that apply to all of the pizza and focaccia recipes:

- People tend to think of pizzas as round and focaccias as rectangles or squares, but focaccias can be round and pizzas can be square or rectangular.

- For square or rectangular pizzas, you can shape the crust in a 12-inch square pan or on a 13 by 18-inch baking sheet. Note that it should only cover about half of the larger pan. If you'd like to make a larger pizza, simply double the recipe.

- For round focaccias, use 2 pie pans or round cake pans, anywhere from 8 to 10 inches across and either 1 or 2 inches deep.

- All of the focaccia doughs call for egg whites beaten until soft peaks form. They'll foam up much more quickly if you bring the egg whites to room temperature first.

- We've suggested specific toppings for the various focaccias, but feel free to mix and match toppings and crusts. Cheese is optional, but if you do use it, try experimenting with other melting cheeses beyond mozzarella, such as provolone, fontina, or even Monterey Jack. Of course, sliced tomatoes and pesto are always delicious toppings.

- All of the pizza crusts must be baked prior to topping so they'll firm up and support the toppings. Also note that they bake at a much lower temperature than conventional crusts in order to crisp the crust without browning it too quickly.

- Once the crusts are baked, making pizzas is a snap. So after you've mastered a given recipe, consider doubling or tripling the batch and baking up the extra crusts for later. Wrap them well and store them in the refrigerator, where they'll keep for up to 3 days, or in the freezer, where they'll keep for at least 3 months.

- A fun shaping option is to make personal-size crusts in small pie or tart pans. Then everyone can choose his or her own toppings. These smaller crusts are also especially easy to store in the freezer.

- If the pizza has toppings on it, you can store it in the refrigerator the same way you would any leftover pizza. When ready to serve, pop into a microwave for about 30 to 60 seconds or place in a 400°F (204°C) oven for about 5 minutes. The oven method will add some crunch back into the edges of the leftover pizza.

Basic Pizza Crust

MAKES ONE 12-INCH PIZZA CRUST

This is our most basic pizza dough, making it the perfect canvas for featuring your favorite toppings. See pages 69 and 71 for a basic tomato sauce and a pesto recipe, and check out the sidebar on page 78 for more topping ideas.

2¼ teaspoons (1 package) instant or active dry yeast

¼ cup (2 oz / 57 g) warm water (about 95°F, or 35°C)

2 cups (8 oz / 227 g) almond flour

½ cup (2 oz / 57 g) sesame seed flour

2 teaspoons Splenda or Stevia Extract in the Raw, or 1 teaspoon New Roots Stevia Sugar

1 teaspoon baking powder

½ teaspoon salt

1 egg (1.75 oz / 50 g)

Preheat the oven to 300°F (163°C). Mist a 12-inch round pizza pan or, for a thinner crust, a 12-inch square baking pan with spray oil.

In a small bowl, stir the yeast and water together until the yeast dissolves. In a medium bowl, combine the almond flour, sesame seed flour, sweetener, baking powder, and salt and whisk until well mixed. Whisk the egg, then add it and the yeast mixture to the flour mixture and stir with a large spoon for 1 to 2 minutes to make a thick, sticky batter (see page 27).

Transfer the dough to the center of the prepared pan. Using oiled fingers, press it out to evenly fill the pan, making the edges slightly thicker if you like.

Prick the surface with a fork every 1 to 2 inches to help prevent bubbles and air pockets during baking. Bake for 15 minutes, then rotate and bake for 10 minutes, just until the dough firms up and starts to brown.

You can immediately top the crust with your favorite toppings or top it later. To bake the topped pizza, preheat the oven to 325°F (204°C). Bake for 6 to 10 minutes, until any cheese has melted or until the toppings are heated through and cooked to your liking. Slice and serve immediately.

Cheesy Herbed Pizza Crust

MAKES ONE 12-INCH PIZZA CRUST

The allure of this recipe is the embedded cheese, along with the rich flavor imparted by chicken or vegetable broth. In fact, this crust can be eaten without any toppings as a delicious herbed cheese crisp, but it's even better with your favorite pizza toppings. (For topping ideas, see page 78). Be sure to have about 1 tablespoon olive oil on hand for dipping your fingers prior to shaping your pizza crust.

1 cup (4 oz / 113 g) sunflower seed flour

1/2 cup (2 oz / 57 g) soy flour, garbanzo bean flour (see Tip, page 38), or almond flour

1 teaspoon baking powder

3/4 teaspoon onion powder

1/2 teaspoon salt

1/2 teaspoon ground black pepper
1/2 teaspoon dried oregano

1/4 teaspoon dried thyme

1/4 cup (1 oz / 28 g) shredded or grated mozzarella cheese

1/4 cup (1 oz / 28 g) shredded or grated Cheddar cheese

2 egg whites (2.5 oz / 71 g)

1/2 cup (4 oz / 113 g) low-sodium chicken broth, vegetable broth, or water

Preheat the oven to 325°F (163°C). Brush the surface of a 12-inch round pizza pan with olive oil.

In a medium bowl, combine the sunflower seed flour, soy flour, baking powder, onion powder, salt, pepper, oregano, and thyme and whisk until well mixed. Stir in the cheeses and stir the mixture to distribute the cheese. In a separate medium bowl, whisk the egg whites and broth together until thoroughly blended. Add the flour mixture and stir with a large spoon for 1 to 2 minutes to make a thick, sticky dough (see page 27).

Transfer the dough to the center of the prepared pan. Using oiled fingers, press it out to evenly fill the pan, making the edges slightly thicker if you like. Prick the surface every 1 to 2 inches to help prevent bubbles and air pockets during baking. Bake for 15 minutes, then rotate and bake for 15 to 20 minutes, until lightly browned and firm to the touch, with blisters of melted cheese all over.

You can immediately top the crust with your favorite toppings or top it later. To bake the topped pizza, preheat the oven to 325°F (163°C). Bake for 6 to 8 minutes, until any cheese has melted or until the toppings are heated through and cooked to your liking. Slice and serve immediately.

Tomato-Basil Pizza Crust

MAKES ONE 12-INCH PIZZA CRUST

This crust is easy to make and has traditional pizza flavors baked right in, so you can even eat it as pizza bread, without toppings and perhaps dipped in marinara sauce. Of course, it's also excellent with toppings. We recommend caramelized onions or sautéed or roasted bell peppers. (For more topping ideas, see page 78.)

1 cup (4 oz / 113 g) sunflower seed flour

1/2 cup (2 oz / 57 g) soy flour or almond flour

1 teaspoon baking powder

1 teaspoon salt

1 1/2 teaspoons dried basil

1 1/2 teaspoons minced fresh garlic, or 3/4 teaspoon granulated garlic

1/4 teaspoon crushed red pepper flakes

2 egg whites (2.5 oz / 71 g)

1/2 cup (4 oz / 113 g) tomato juice

Preheat the oven to 325°F (163°C). Mist a 12-inch round pizza pan or, for a thinner crust, a 12-inch square baking pan with spray oil.

In a medium bowl, combine the sunflower seed flour, soy flour, baking powder, salt, basil, garlic, and red pepper flakes and whisk until well mixed. In a separate medium bowl, whisk the egg whites and tomato juice together until thoroughly blended. Add the flour mixture and stir with a large spoon for 1 to 2 minutes to make a thick, sticky batter (see page 27).

Transfer the dough to the center of the prepared pan. Using oiled fingers, press it out to evenly fill the pan, making the edges slightly thicker if you like.

Prick the surface with a fork every 1 to 2 inches to help prevent bubbles and air pockets during baking. Bake for 15 minutes, then rotate and bake for 10 minutes, just until the dough firms up and starts to brown.

You can immediately top the crust with your favorite toppings or top it later. To bake the topped pizza, preheat the oven to 325°F (163°C). Bake for 6 to 10 minutes, until any cheese has melted or until the toppings are heated through and cooked to your liking. Slice and serve immediately.

Herbed Tomato Sauce

MAKES 3½ CUPS; ENOUGH FOR 4 TO 6 PIZZAS OR FOCACCIAS

You can use store-bought marinara sauce or other tomato sauces for pizzas and focaccias. But if you would like to make your own, the flavors will be fresher and brighter; plus, you can tweak them to your liking. Here's our favorite recipe for a crushed tomato sauce, from Peter's book *American Pie: My Search for the Perfect Pizza*. This sauce couldn't be easier to put together. It doesn't even require any cooking, as the canned tomatoes are already cooked and the sauce will be heated during baking. The flavors of the herbs and garlic will intensify during baking, so resist the urge to add more. If you'd like to use this sauce with pasta, simply heat it in a saucepan.

1 can (28 oz / 794 g) crushed, ground, or whole plum tomatoes

1 to 2 tablespoons red wine vinegar, balsamic vinegar, fresh lemon juice, or a combination (optional)

1 tablespoon granulated garlic, or 5 cloves garlic, minced or crushed

1 teaspoon dried basil, or 2 tablespoons minced fresh basil (optional)

1 teaspoon dried oregano, or 1 tablespoon minced fresh oregano (optional)

¼ teaspoon coarsely ground black pepper

½ teaspoon salt, or more as needed

In a medium bowl, combine the tomatoes, vinegar, garlic, basil, oregano, pepper, and salt. Taste and add more salt as desired; the amount needed will vary depending on the brand of tomatoes used. Stored in an airtight container, the sauce will keep for 1 week in the refrigerator or 3 months in the freezer.

Basil Pesto

MAKES ABOUT 3 CUPS; ENOUGH FOR ABOUT 6 PIZZAS OR FOCACCIAS

Pesto is a sprightly sauce to use on pizza and focaccia, and with many other dishes as well. This is Peter's favorite version, but feel free to play with the recipe. To get you started, we've included several variations. Just one caveat: Don't use packaged grated cheese. For optimum flavor and best results, the cheese should be freshly grated.

1 tablespoon olive oil

8 cloves garlic, coarsely chopped

2 cups tightly packed fresh basil leaves

1 cup (8 oz / 227 g) extra-virgin olive oil, or as needed

1 cup (4.75 oz / 135 g) pine nuts, lightly toasted (see Tip, page 172)

3/4 cup (2.5 oz / 71 g) freshly grated Parmesan, Romano, Asiago, or Grana Padano cheese

1 1/2 tablespoons fresh lemon juice

Heat the 1 tablespoon olive oil in a small skillet over medium-high heat. Add the garlic and sauté for about 20 seconds, just to help tame the flavor. Immediately transfer the garlic and oil to a separate dish.

Put the basil, 1 cup olive oil, pine nuts, Parmesan, and lemon juice in a food processor. Add the garlic and its cooking oil and process until smooth. The pesto should be thick but spreadable. If it's too thick, add more olive oil; if it's too thin, add more cheese.

Stored in an airtight container in the refrigerator, the pesto will keep for about 1 week. If the top surface darkens, this is just oxidation—simply stir the dark layer on top back into the bright green pesto underneath. If you freeze pesto, it will remain bright green until you thaw it, but then it will darken throughout (more oxidation). You can still use it, but it won't be as vibrant looking. Still, dark pesto is better than no pesto at all, and you can brighten it up by stirring in a little more lemon juice.

VARIATIONS

Walnut or Pecan Pesto: Substitute toasted walnuts or pecans for the pine nuts.

Herb Pesto: Replace the basil with other mild fresh herbs, such as parsley or cilantro, or even arugula. You can also substitute fresh herbs with a stronger flavor, such as oregano or marjoram, in which case you should use much less; try about ¼ cup along with 1¾ cup of a milder herb like fresh basil or Italian parsley. Another option is to use a blend of fresh herbs.

Roasted Red Bell Pepper Pesto: Substitute roasted red bell peppers for the basil.

Chunky Pesto: Hold back half of the pine nuts and cheese and fold them into the pesto after it has been processed. This adds both texture and little bursts of flavor from the toasted nuts and salty cheese.

Olive Oil and Two-Basil Focaccia

MAKES ONE 9 BY 13-INCH FOCACCIA

Of the five gluten-free, sugar-free focaccia recipes we offer in this book, this one is most similar to traditional wheat flour versions featuring an herbed oil topping. The high proportion of flaxseed meal gives it a creamy interior texture, along with a wide array of nutritional benefits. We call for both dried and fresh basil in the herbed oil because each adds distinctive flavor characteristics. It doesn't really need any topping beyond what is called for, but as with all focaccias, you can add any number of other toppings. (For tips on topping focaccia with cheese, see page 78.)

Basil Herbed Oil

1/4 cup (2 oz / 57 g) extra-virgin olive oil

2 tablespoons minced or slivered fresh basil

1 1/2 teaspoons coarse sea salt or kosher salt

1 tablespoon dried basil

1 teaspoon ground black pepper

Dough

1 1/2 cups (6 oz / 170 g) golden flaxseed meal

1 1/2 cups (6 oz / 170 g) almond flour

2 teaspoons baking powder

1/2 teaspoon xanthan gum

1/2 teaspoon salt

1 cup (8 oz / 227 g) unsweetened soy milk or other milk

1/8 teaspoon liquid stevia

4 egg whites (5 oz / 142 g), at room temperature

Preheat the oven to 400°F (204°C). Line a 9 by 13-inch baking pan with parchment paper or a silicone mat, then mist the bottom and sides with spray oil (preferably olive oil cooking spray).

To make the herbed oil, combine all of the ingredients in a small bowl and whisk until thoroughly combined.

To make the dough, combine the flaxseed meal, almond flour, baking powder, xanthan gum, and salt in a large bowl and whisk until well mixed. In a small bowl or measuring cup, stir the milk and liquid stevia together.

Put the egg whites in a medium bowl. Using an electric mixer with the whisk attachment at medium-high speed (or a strong arm with a sturdy whisk—and good endurance), beat the eggs for 3 to 5 minutes, until fairly stiff peaks form.

Add the milk mixture to the flour mixture and stir to make a smooth batter. Gently fold in the egg whites with a rubber spatula, deflating the egg whites as little as possible to make a smooth, sticky dough that is slightly fluffy (see page 27).   (CONTINUED)

To assemble and bake the focaccia, gently transfer the dough to the prepared pan, then spread it in an even layer with a spatula. Dip your fingers into the herbed oil, then dimple the dough all over the top. Drizzle the herbed oil evenly over the surface.

Bake for 20 minutes, then rotate and bake for 20 to 25 minutes, until golden brown on top and springy when pressed in the center.

Let the focaccia cool for about 5 minutes before removing it from the pan, cutting it into portions, and serving.

Rosemary and Olive Oil Focaccia

MAKES ONE 9 BY 13-INCH FOCACCIA

This simple, basic recipe uses only one type of flour: almond flour. The rosemary herbed oil is just like the classic version that hails from Genoa and is so often used on traditional focaccias. As the Italians have taught us, simple is good, especially when cooking with high-quality ingredients. This focaccia is excellent by itself or served as a table bread and can also be used as a dipping bread for marinara sauce or herb oil, or for panini filled with your favorite sandwich fixings. You can also add other toppings if you like. (For tips on topping focaccia with cheese, see page 78.)

Rosemary Herbed Oil

1/4 cup (2 oz / 57 g) extra-virgin olive oil

2 teaspoons minced fresh rosemary

1 teaspoon salt

1/2 teaspoon ground black pepper

Dough

3 cups (12 oz / 340 g) almond flour

2 teaspoons baking powder

1/2 teaspoon xanthan gum

1/2 teaspoon salt

4 egg whites (5 oz / 142 g), at room temperature

1 cup (8 oz / 227 g) unsweetened soy milk or other milk

Preheat the oven to 400°F (204°C). Line a 9 by 13-inch baking pan with parchment paper or a silicone mat, then mist the bottom and sides with spray oil (preferably olive oil cooking spray).

To make the herbed oil, combine all of the ingredients in a small bowl and whisk until thoroughly combined.

To make the dough, combine the almond flour, baking powder, xanthan gum, and salt in a large bowl and whisk until well mixed.

Put the egg whites in a medium bowl. Using an electric mixer with the whisk attachment at medium-high speed (or a strong arm with a sturdy whisk—and good endurance), beat the eggs for 3 to 5 minutes, until fairly stiff peaks form.

Add the milk to the flour mixture and stir to make a smooth batter. Gently fold in the egg whites with a rubber spatula, deflating the egg whites as little as possible to make a smooth, sticky dough that is slightly fluffy (see page 27). (CONTINUED)

To assemble and bake the focaccia, gently transfer the dough to the prepared pan, then spread it in an even layer with a spatula. Dip your fingers into the herbed oil, then dimple the dough all over the top. Drizzle the herbed oil evenly over the surface.

Bake for 25 minutes, then rotate and bake for 20 to 25 minutes, until golden brown on top and springy when pressed in the center.

Let the focaccia cool for about 5 minutes before removing it from the pan, cutting it into portions, and serving.

Olive Oil and Parsley Focaccia

MAKES ONE 9 BY 13-INCH FOCACCIA

Garbanzo bean flour provides a nice, flaky texture, along with a good amount of protein and fiber. The olive oil and parsley topping is simple yet very tasty; however, you can certainly add other toppings if you like. (For tips on topping focaccia with cheese, see page 78.)

Parsley Herbed Oil

1/4 cup (2 oz / 57 g) extra-virgin olive oil

1 1/2 teaspoons sea salt or coarse kosher salt

1/2 teaspoon dried parsley, or 1 tablespoon minced fresh parsley

1/4 teaspoon ground black pepper

Dough

2 cups (8 oz / 227 g) almond flour

1 cup (4 oz / 113 g) garbanzo bean flour (see Tip, page 38)

2 teaspoons baking powder

1 teaspoon salt

1/2 teaspoon xanthan gum

4 egg whites (5 oz / 142 g), at room temperature

1 cup (8 oz / 227 g) chicken broth, vegetable broth, or water

Preheat the oven to 400°F (204°C). Line a 9 by 13-inch baking pan with parchment paper or a silicone mat, then mist the bottom and sides with spray oil (preferably olive oil cooking spray).

To make the herbed oil, combine all of the ingredients in a small bowl and whisk until thoroughly combined.

To make the dough, combine the almond flour, garbanzo bean flour, baking powder, xanthan gum, and salt in a large bowl and whisk until well mixed.

Put the egg whites in a medium bowl. Using an electric mixer with the whisk attachment at medium-high speed (or a strong arm with a sturdy whisk—and good endurance), beat the eggs for 3 to 5 minutes, until fairly stiff peaks form.

Add the broth to the flour mixture and stir to make a smooth batter. Gently fold in the egg whites with a rubber spatula, deflating the egg whites as little as possible to make a smooth, sticky dough that is slightly fluffy (see page 27).

To assemble and bake the focaccia, gently transfer the dough to the prepared pan, then spread it in an even layer with a spatula. Dip your fingers into the herbed oil, then dimple the dough all over the top. Drizzle the herbed oil evenly over the surface. (CONTINUED)

Bake for 25 minutes, then rotate and bake for 20 to 25 minutes, until golden brown on top and springy when pressed in the center.

Let the focaccia cool for about 5 minutes before removing it from the pan, cutting it into portions, and serving.

Other Pizza and Focaccia Toppings

The tomato sauce and pesto recipes in this chapter are from Peter's book *American Pie: My Search for the Perfect Pizza.* That book includes many other recipes and ideas for toppings, and most of them would be great on these gluten-free, sugar-free crusts. We'll share a few more ideas below, but if pizza is your thing, you might want to pick up a copy of Peter's book, even if you can't have the wheat flour crusts. For more on pizza and focaccia, including recipes and videos, also check out www.pizzaquest.com, a website hosted by Peter.

Almost any savory ingredient is fair game for a pizza topping. It really comes down to personal preference, so we encourage you to experiment and discover your favorite combinations. The possibilities are genuinely endless. Here are just a few tips.

- Because the pizza crusts in this book are prebaked, after you apply the toppings they cook for less than 10 minutes. That means you can apply any cheese just before baking the pizza.

- Because the baking time for focaccia is longer, you need to hold off on adding cheese until shortly before it comes out of the oven. For softer, moist cheeses, such as mozzarella or provolone, scatter 1 cup (4 oz / 113 g) of shredded or grated cheese evenly over the top about 5 minutes before the focaccia is finished baking. For hard, aged cheeses, such as Parmesan or Asiago, wait until the focaccia is fully baked, then sprinkle about 1 cup (3.5 oz / 99 g) of grated hard cheese over the top and bake for 2 to 3 minutes, just until the cheese melts.

- Mozzarella, Provolone, Parmesan, and other Italian cheeses are classic choices for pizza and focaccia toppings, but if you have other favorites or want to experiment, there is only one rule to follow: the flavor rule (that is, flavor rules!). Why not try Cheddar, Fontina, Swiss, or even Monterey Jack? Let your palate (and any dietary restrictions) be your guide.

- Raw vegetables such as bell peppers, mushrooms, and even onions can sometimes become rubbery or burn when baked on top. To avoid this, first lightly sauté them in olive oil or vegetable oil. Always taste your toppings before putting them on, and adjust the seasonings as you see fit. Sometimes just a bit of salt or pepper can really make the flavors pop.

Double-Cheese Focaccia with Tomato Sauce

MAKES ONE 9 BY 13-INCH FOCACCIA

This focaccia is very much like what New Yorkers call either a Grandma pizza or a Sicilian pizza. It's cheesy and saucy and will bring back fond memories if you grew up with those neighborhood classics. One of its unique characteristics is the use of cheese both in the dough and as a topping. However, if you aren't a cheese lover, you can make the dough without the cheese and forgo the cheese on top. This makes it a marinara focaccia, which is also quite delicious.

Tomato Sauce

1/4 cup (2 oz / 57 g) tomato puree or tomato sauce

1/4 cup (2 oz / 57 g) extra-virgin olive oil

1 tablespoon minced fresh garlic

1 teaspoon ground black pepper

1/2 teaspoon salt, or to taste

Dough

2 cups (8 oz / 227 g) almond flour

1 cup (4 oz / 113 g) sunflower seed flour

2 teaspoons baking powder

1/2 teaspoon xanthan gum

1/4 teaspoon salt

4 egg whites (5 oz / 142 g), at room temperature

1 cup (8 oz / 227 g) chicken broth or vegetable broth

3/4 cup (3 oz / 85 g) grated mozzarella, fontina, or Monterey Jack cheese, plus 3/4 cup for topping

Preheat the oven to 400°F (204°C). Line a 9 by 13-inch baking pan with parchment paper or a silicone mat, then mist the bottom and sides with spray oil (preferably olive oil cooking spray).

To make the sauce, combine the tomato puree, olive oil, garlic, and pepper in a small bowl and whisk until thoroughly combined. Taste and add salt as needed; if using tomato puree you will probably need as much as ½ teaspoon, but if using tomato sauce you may not need any salt, depending on the brand.

To make the dough, combine the almond flour, sunflower seed flour, baking powder, xanthan gum, and salt in a large bowl and whisk until well mixed.   (CONTINUED)

Put the egg whites in a medium bowl. Using an electric mixer with the whisk attachment at medium-high speed (or a strong arm with a sturdy whisk—and good endurance), beat the eggs for 3 to 5 minutes, until fairly stiff peaks form.

Add the broth to the flour mixture and stir to make a smooth batter. Fold in ¾ cup of the cheese, then gently fold in the egg whites with a rubber spatula, deflating the egg whites as little as possible to make a smooth, sticky dough that is slightly fluffy (see page 27).

To assemble and bake the focaccia, gently transfer the dough to the prepared pan, then spread it in an even layer with a spatula. Oil your fingertips, then dimple the dough all over the top. Spread the sauce evenly over the surface.

Bake for 25 minutes, then rotate and bake for 20 to 25 minutes, until springy when pressed in the center. During the last 5 minutes of baking, sprinkle the remaining ¾ cup cheese over the top.

Let the focaccia cool for about 5 minutes before removing it from the pan, cutting it into portions, and serving.

Focaccia with Herbed Tapenade

MAKES ONE 9 BY 13-INCH FOCACCIA

A fun and easy way to concoct an elaborate topping is to incorporate a prepared ingredient, such as tapenade. Tapenade is traditionally a spread made from olive oil and minced olives, capers, and even anchovies, but in recent years the term has been stretched to embrace a wide variety of ingredients prepared in the classic style. Sun-dried tomatoes, roasted red bell peppers, and artichoke hearts are three popular versions. There are many recipes for these on the Internet, but there's no reason you can't buy a high-quality brand, such as Bella Cucina or Trader Joe's, and save yourself some work. If you'd like to add cheese to the toppings, see page 78 for tips on when to add it.

Herbed Tapenade Topping

- 1/2 cup artichoke tapenade or other commercial tapenade, or to taste
- 1/4 cup (2 oz / 57 g) extra-virgin olive oil
- 1/2 teaspoon salt
- 1 teaspoon dried basil
- 1 teaspoon dried parsley, or 2 tablespoons minced fresh parsley
- 1/2 teaspoon ground black pepper
- 1/8 teaspoon dried oregano

Dough

- 2 cups (8 oz / 227 g) almond flour
- 1 cup (4 oz / 113 g) golden or brown flaxseed meal
- 2 teaspoons baking powder
- 1/2 teaspoon xanthan gum
- 1/2 teaspoon salt
- 1 cup (8 oz / 227 g) unsweetened soy milk or other milk
- 1/8 teaspoon liquid stevia
- 4 egg whites (5 oz / 142 g), at room temperature

Preheat the oven to 400°F (204°C). Line a 9 by 13-inch baking pan with parchment paper or a silicone mat, then mist the bottom and sides with spray oil (preferably olive oil cooking spray).

To make the topping, combine all of the ingredients in a small bowl and stir until thoroughly combined.

To make the dough, combine the almond flour, flaxseed meal, baking powder, xanthan gum, and salt in a large bowl and whisk until well mixed. In a small bowl or measuring cup, stir the milk and liquid stevia together.

Put the egg whites in a medium bowl. Using an electric mixer with the whisk attachment at medium-high speed (or a strong arm with a sturdy whisk—and good endurance), beat the eggs for 3 to 5 minutes, until fairly stiff peaks form.

Add the milk mixture to the flour mixture and stir to make a smooth batter. Gently fold in the egg whites with a rubber spatula, deflating the egg whites as little as possible to make a smooth, sticky dough that is slightly fluffy (see page 27).

To assemble and bake the focaccia, gently transfer the dough to the prepared pan, then spread it in an even layer with a spatula. Oil your fingertips, then dimple the dough all over the top. Spread the topping evenly over the surface.

Bake for 25 minutes, then rotate and bake for 20 to 25 minutes, until springy when pressed in the center.

Let the focaccia cool for about 5 minutes before removing it from the pan, cutting it into portions, and serving.

Chapter Three

CRACKERS, BREADSTICKS, AND PRETZELS

This chapter consists of three very similar and basic doughs tweaked into a multitude of savory treats by adding a variety of flavorful ingredients and seasonings. As you will see once you make a few of these recipes, they are extremely versatile. Soon you'll be developing your own unique variations using different combinations of seed and nut flours and different flavorings.

In all of their endless variations, these crispy baked delights can be eaten in a multitude of ways: with dips and spreads, alongside soups or salads, with a main course, or as appetizers—either alone or with accompaniments. For breadsticks, a fun idea is serving them with marinara sauce or a flavored herb oil for dipping. All of the items in this chapter are also a tasty and healthy alternative to potato chips, corn chips, and other commercial snack foods, so be sure to bake them up regularly and keep them on hand for those times when you need a little nibble.

These crackers are fine without an egg wash, but you can certainly use an egg wash (as described on page 86) to add a sheen or help toppings adhere; however, egg replacer can't be used for the egg wash, so forgo that step if you don't want to use eggs.

For optimum crispness, let crackers cool completely before serving them. Breadsticks and pretzels may be served warm, at room temperature, or cold. You can store crackers and pretzels in an airtight container in the pantry for up to 1 week. Just make sure they are completely cooled before sealing in the airtight container.

One final note: As a reminder, when using commercially ground pecan flour (or pecan meal) instead of home-ground pecan flour, you may have to increase the amount of liquid if the dough doesn't come together to make a thick, sticky batter. You can add water to the batter, 1 teaspoon at a time, or, if the dough is very dry and crumbly, you can use egg or egg whites for the additional liquid. If you need to adjust the liquid for crackers, we suggest adding either a whole egg or an ounce or two of egg whites (a large egg has about 1 ounce to $1\frac{1}{4}$ ounces of egg white, or you can measure it from a carton). Add only enough to get the job done, and only if needed. For breadsticks and any recipes that call for liquids such as milk or water, simply add more liquid, if needed, up to $\frac{1}{4}$ cup of additional liquid per cup of pecan flour.

Simple Crackers

These are the most versatile crackers in this chapter. They can be served alongside almost any savory dish or be topped with almost anything, or you can simply eat them on their own. They have an enticing buttery flavor and a texture that crumbles and melts in your mouth. As you'll see in the sidebar on page 93, the potential variations are endless.

3 cups (12 oz / 340 g) almond flour

1 tablespoon Splenda or Stevia Extract in the Raw, or 1½ teaspoons New Roots Stevia Sugar

1 teaspoon baking powder

1 teaspoon salt

1 egg (1.75 oz / 50 g)

¼ cup (2 oz / 57 g) salted butter or margarine, melted

Egg Wash (optional)

1 egg (1.75 oz / 50 g)

2 tablespoons water

Position 2 racks in the center of the oven. Preheat the oven to 300°F (149°C). Cover 2 baking sheets with parchment paper or silicone mats, then lightly mist the surfaces with spray oil.

In a medium bowl, combine the almond flour, sweetener, baking powder, and salt and whisk until well mixed. In a large bowl, whisk the egg and butter together until thoroughly blended. Add the flour mixture and stir with a large spoon until all of the ingredients are thoroughly combined. The dough will be stiff. Scrape down the sides of the bowl and form the dough into a ball; if it's too dry to form a ball, stir in a bit of water, 1 teaspoon at a time, just until the dough comes together and all of the loose flour is incorporated, to make a stiff, playdough-like dough (see page 27).

Mist 2 pieces of parchment paper or 2 silicone mats with spray oil. Place the dough between the oiled surfaces, then use a rolling pin to roll and flatten the dough until slightly thinner than ¼ inch.

Put a bit of vegetable oil in a saucer or small, shallow dish. Dip a 2-inch round biscuit cutter into the oil to coat the cutting edge. Gently peel back the top piece of parchment or silicone mat and cut the crackers.

Peel the cut pieces off the parchment with either your hands or a small metal spatula and transfer them to the prepared pans. They won't spread, so you can position them fairly close to each other, nearly touching. Gather any scraps, roll them out, and cut more crackers until all of the dough has been used.

Make the egg wash by whisking the egg and water together until frothy, then brush the mixture over the crackers. (If adding toppings, as suggested in the sidebar on page 93, sprinkle them over the crackers now.)

Bake for 15 minutes, then rotate the pans and switch racks and bake for 15 to 20 minutes, until the crackers are golden brown and crisp. Thicker crackers may require longer baking.

Immediately transfer the crackers to a wire rack to cool completely. They will get crispier as they cool.

Garlic Crackers

MAKES 36 TO 42 TWO-INCH ROUND CRACKERS

Garlic has a wonderful flavor and, as a bonus, its aroma stimulates the senses. This cracker capitalizes on those qualities and also includes black pepper for extra zing. Once you've tried this recipe, use the sidebar on page 93 to create your own variations!

2 cups (8 oz / 227 g) almond flour

1 cup (4 oz / 113 g) pecan flour (see page 85)

1 tablespoon Splenda or Stevia Extract in the Raw, or 1½ teaspoons New Roots Stevia Sugar

1 teaspoon baking powder

1 teaspoon salt

1 tablespoon minced fresh garlic

½ to 1 teaspoon ground black pepper

1 egg (1.75 oz / 50 g)

¼ cup (2 oz / 57 g) salted butter or margarine, melted

Egg Wash (optional)

1 egg (1.75 oz / 50 g)

2 tablespoons water

Position 2 racks in the center of the oven. Preheat the oven to 300°F (149°C). Cover 2 baking sheets with parchment paper or silicone mats, then lightly mist the surfaces with spray oil.

In a medium bowl, combine the almond flour, pecan flour, sweetener, baking powder, salt, garlic, and pepper and whisk until well mixed. In a large bowl, whisk the egg and butter together until thoroughly blended. Add the flour mixture and stir with a large spoon until all of the ingredients are thoroughly combined. The dough will be stiff. Scrape down the sides of the bowl and form the dough into a ball; if it's too dry to form a ball, stir in a bit of water, 1 teaspoon at a time, just until the dough comes together and all of the loose flour is incorporated to make a stiff, playdough-like dough (see page 27).

Mist 2 pieces of parchment paper or 2 silicone mats with spray oil. Place the dough between the oiled surfaces, then use a rolling pin to roll and flatten the dough until slightly thinner than ¼ inch.

Put a bit of vegetable oil in a saucer or small, shallow dish. Dip a 2-inch round biscuit cutter into the oil to coat the cutting edge. Gently peel back the top piece of parchment or silicone mat and cut the crackers.

Peel the cut pieces off the parchment with either your hands or a small metal spatula and transfer them to the prepared pans. They won't spread, so you can position them quite close to each other, nearly touching. Gather any scraps, roll them out, and cut more crackers until all of the dough has been used.

Make the egg wash by whisking the egg and water together until frothy, then brush the mixture over the crackers. (If adding toppings, as suggested in the sidebar on page 93, sprinkle them over the crackers now.)

Bake for 15 minutes, then rotate the pans and switch racks and bake for 15 to 20 minutes, until the crackers are golden brown and crisp. Thicker crackers may require longer baking.

Immediately transfer the crackers to a wire rack to cool completely. They will get crispier as they cool.

Rosemary Crackers

MAKES 36 TO 42 TWO-INCH ROUND CRACKERS

This zesty cracker is seasoned with a mixture of rosemary and just a spark of cayenne pepper. If you prefer a different herb, use basil or any savory herb. Feel free to play with the flour blend. As long as the total amount is 3 cups (340 g), you can use any combination you like, including using more than two flours. Pumpkin seed or hemp seed meal would work well in place of the sesame seed flour. For more tips on variations, see the sidebar on page 93.

2 cups (8 oz / 227 g) almond flour

1 cup (4 oz / 113 g) sesame seed flour

1 tablespoon Splenda or Stevia Extract in the Raw, or 1¹⁄₂ teaspoons New Roots Stevia Sugar

1 teaspoon baking powder

1 teaspoon salt

2 teaspoons minced fresh rosemary

¹⁄₂ teaspoon cayenne pepper

1 egg (1.75 oz / 50 g)

¹⁄₄ cup (2 oz / 57 g) salted butter or margarine, melted

Egg Wash (optional)

1 egg (1.75 oz / 50 g)

2 tablespoons water

Position 2 racks in the center of the oven. Preheat the oven to 300°F (149°C). Cover 2 baking sheets with parchment paper or silicone mats, then lightly mist the surfaces with spray oil.

In a medium bowl, combine the almond flour, sesame seed flour, sweetener, baking powder, salt, rosemary, and cayenne and whisk until well mixed. In a large bowl, whisk the egg and butter together until thoroughly blended. Add the flour mixture and stir with a large spoon until all of the ingredients are thoroughly combined. The dough will be stiff. Scrape down the sides of the bowl and form the dough into a ball; if it's too dry to form a ball, stir in a bit of water, 1 teaspoon at a time, just until the dough comes together and all of the loose flour is incorporated to make a stiff, playdough-like dough (see page 27).

Mist 2 pieces of parchment paper or 2 silicone mats with spray oil. Place the dough between the oiled surfaces, then use a rolling pin to roll and flatten the dough until slightly thinner than ¼ inch.   (CONTINUED)

Put a bit of vegetable oil in a saucer or small, shallow dish. Dip a 2-inch round biscuit cutter into the oil to coat the cutting edge. Gently peel back the top piece of parchment or silicone mat and cut the crackers.

Peel the cut pieces off the parchment with either your hands or a small metal spatula and transfer them to the prepared pans. They won't spread, so you can position them quite close to each other, nearly touching. Gather any scraps, roll them out, and cut more crackers until all of the dough has been used.

Make the egg wash by whisking the egg and water together until frothy, then brush the mixture over the crackers. (If adding toppings, as suggested in the sidebar on page 93, sprinkle them over the crackers now.)

Bake for 15 minutes, then rotate the pans and switch racks and bake for 15 to 20 minutes, until the crackers are golden brown and crisp. Thicker crackers may require longer baking.

Immediately transfer the crackers to a wire rack to cool completely. They will get crispier as they cool.

VARIATION

Herb Crackers: Add 1 teaspoon dried basil (or 2 tablespoons minced fresh basil), ½ teaspoon ground black pepper, ¼ teaspoon dried thyme, and ⅛ teaspoon dried oregano when mixing the dry ingredients.

Cracker Variations

Here are a few ideas for creating your own variations of any of the cracker recipes in this chapter:

- Use different types of nut and seed flours in different proportions. Any combination is fine, as long as the total amount is equal to what's called for in the recipe.

- For zesty crackers, add 1/4 teaspoon of white pepper or cayenne when mixing the dry ingredients.

- For sesame crackers, toast 2 tablespoons of sesame seeds (see Tip, page 172), then add them to the dry ingredients.

- Most of the cracker recipes call for melted butter, but you can certainly substitute olive oil.

- To make cheese crackers, add 1/2 cup (about 2 oz / 57 g) of finely grated cheese (any variety) when mixing the dry ingredients.

- These recipes call for using a 2-inch round biscuit or cookie cutter, but you can use any shape of cutter you like, or cut free-form crackers with a pizza cutter. One advantage to using a pizza cutter is that it avoids the trouble of gathering and rerolling the scraps of dough. Plus, you can brush the egg wash over the surface and sprinkle on any toppings before cutting out the crackers—much easier than egg washing each individual cracker.

- Once the crackers are rolled out and brushed with egg wash, sprinkle various enhancements over the top. The possibilities are endless: try Maldon or coarse salt, garlic salt or granulated garlic, seasoned salt, black pepper, paprika, crushed red pepper flakes, dried basil, dried parsley, minced garlic, sesame seeds, poppy seeds, sunflower seeds, chopped pumpkin seeds, finely chopped pecans or walnuts, or whatever you like! The egg wash will help the toppings stick to the crackers. If you don't use the egg wash, try gently pressing the toppings into the dough so they adhere.

- Crackers made without toppings are also wonderful. The egg wash gives them a nice sheen, so use it even if you aren't adding any toppings.

Onion-Cayenne Crackers

MAKES 36 TO 42 TWO-INCH ROUND CRACKERS

This savory variation on Simple Crackers (page 86) combines the pungency of dried onion with the heat of cayenne pepper. Adjust the amount of cayenne to suit your palate. These crackers are great with stews, soups, or gumbo. As always, feel free to experiment. We've included a couple of variations below, and you can also consult the sidebar on page 93 for more ideas.

3 cups (12 oz / 340 g) almond flour

2 tablespoons Splenda or Stevia Extract in the Raw, or 1 tablespoon New Roots Stevia Sugar

1 teaspoon baking powder

1 teaspoon salt

1 teaspoon onion powder, or 2 tablespoons dried onion flakes

1 teaspoon dried parsley

1/2 to 1 teaspoon ground cayenne pepper

1 egg (1.75 oz / 50 g)

1/4 cup (2 oz / 57 g) salted butter or margarine, melted

Egg Wash (optional)

1 egg (1.75 oz / 50 g)

2 tablespoons water

Position 2 racks in the center of the oven. Preheat the oven to 300°F (149°C). Cover 2 baking sheets with parchment paper or silicone mats, then lightly mist the surfaces with spray oil.

In a medium bowl, combine the almond flour, sweetener, baking powder, salt, onion powder, parsley, and cayenne and whisk until well mixed. In a large bowl, whisk the egg and butter together until thoroughly blended. Add the flour mixture and stir with a large spoon until all of the ingredients are thoroughly combined. The dough will be stiff. Scrape down the sides of the bowl and form the dough into a ball; if it's too dry to form a ball, stir in a bit of water, 1 teaspoon at a time, just until the dough comes together and all of the loose flour is incorporated to make a stiff, playdough-like dough (see page 27).

Mist 2 pieces of parchment paper or 2 silicone mats with spray oil. Place the dough between the oiled surfaces, then use a rolling pin to roll and flatten the dough until slightly thinner than ¼ inch.

Put a bit of vegetable oil in a saucer or small, shallow dish. Dip a 2-inch round biscuit cutter into the oil to coat the cutting edge. Gently peel back the top piece of parchment or silicone mat and cut the crackers.

Peel the cut pieces off the parchment with either your hands or a small metal spatula and transfer them to the prepared pans. They won't spread, so you can position them quite close to each other, nearly touching. Gather any scraps, roll them out, and cut more crackers until all of the dough has been used.

Make the egg wash by whisking the egg and water together until frothy, then brush the mixture over the crackers. (If adding toppings, as suggested in the sidebar on page 93, sprinkle them over the crackers now.)

Bake for 15 minutes, then rotate the pans and switch racks and bake for 15 to 20 minutes, until the crackers are golden brown and crisp. Thicker crackers may require longer baking.

Immediately transfer the crackers to a wire rack to cool completely. They will get crispier as they cool.

VARIATIONS

Two-Pepper Crackers: Use only ½ teaspoon cayenne and add ½ teaspoon white pepper when mixing the dry ingredients.

Onion, Cayenne, and Cheese Crackers: For added flavor, sprinkle a pinch of shredded cheese, or to taste, over the crackers 1 to 2 minutes before they come out of the oven. You can use as much or as little cheese as you want, but use a cheese that melts well, such as Cheddar, Jack, Swiss, fontina, provolone, or mozzarella, not a dry, aged cheese.

Black Pepper and Swiss Cheese Crackers

MAKES 36 TO 42 TWO-INCH ROUND CRACKERS

The combination of black pepper and Swiss cheese evokes memories of cheese fondue. But here, instead of dipping various foods into the melted cheese, you can serve them on top of this cheesy cracker! Feel free to cut the crackers into various decorative shapes and even change up the nut and seed flour combinations. If your diet will allow it, to continue the fondue experience, serve these crackers with a crisp white wine or sauternes.

2 cups (8 oz / 227 g) almond flour

1 cup (4 oz / 113 g) sesame seed flour

1/2 cup (2 oz / 57 g) shredded or grated Emmentaler or Gruyère cheese

1 tablespoon Splenda or Stevia Extract in the Raw, or 1 1/2 teaspoons New Roots Stevia Sugar

1 teaspoon baking powder

1/2 teaspoon salt

1/2 to 1 teaspoon ground black pepper

1 egg (1.75 oz / 50 g)

1/4 cup (2 oz / 57 g) olive oil

Egg Wash (optional)

1 egg (1.75 oz / 50 g)

2 tablespoons water

Position 2 racks in the center of the oven. Preheat the oven to 300°F (149°C). Cover 2 baking sheets with parchment paper or silicone mats, then lightly mist the surfaces with spray oil.

In a medium bowl, combine the almond flour, sesame seed flour, cheese, sweetener, baking powder, salt, and pepper and whisk until well mixed. In a large bowl, whisk the egg and olive oil together until thoroughly blended. Add the flour mixture and stir with a large spoon until all of the ingredients are thoroughly combined. The dough will be stiff. Scrape down the sides of the bowl and form the dough into a ball; if it's too dry to form a ball, stir in a bit of water, 1 teaspoon at a time, just until the dough comes together and all of the loose flour is incorporated, to make a stiff, playdough-like dough (see page 27).

Mist 2 pieces of parchment paper or 2 silicone mats with spray oil. Place the dough between the oiled surfaces, then use a rolling pin to roll and flatten the dough until slightly thinner than 1/4 inch.

Put a bit of vegetable oil in a saucer or small, shallow dish. Dip a 2-inch round biscuit cutter into the oil to coat the cutting edge. Gently peel back the top piece of parchment or silicone mat and cut the crackers.

Peel the cut pieces off the parchment with either your hands or a small metal spatula and transfer them to the prepared pans. They won't spread, so you can position them quite close to each other, nearly touching. Gather any scraps, roll them out, and cut more crackers until all of the dough has been used.

Make the egg wash by whisking the egg and water together until frothy, then brush the mixture over the crackers. (If adding toppings, as suggested in the sidebar on page 93, sprinkle them over the crackers now.)

Bake for 15 minutes, then rotate the pans and switch racks and bake for 15 to 20 minutes, until the crackers are golden brown and crisp. Thicker crackers may require longer baking.

Immediately transfer the crackers to a wire rack to cool completely. They will get crispier as they cool.

Sesame Seed and Mozzarella Crackers

MAKES 36 TWO-INCH ROUND CRACKERS

Sesame seed flour is perfect for crackers, as it helps them bake up nice and crispy. Plus, the combination of sesame seed flour as the primary flour and almond flour in support makes for a robust blend of flavors. Adding a cheese that melts well, such as mozzarella, fontina, Monterey Jack, or even Cheddar, takes these crackers to an even higher level.

1½ cups (6 ounces / 170 g) sesame seed flour

½ cup (2 oz / 57 g) almond flour

1 teaspoon baking powder

¾ teaspoon salt

½ teaspoon onion powder

½ teaspoon ground black pepper

2 eggs (3.5 oz / 99 g)

1 cup (4 oz / 113 g) shredded or grated low-moisture mozzarella cheese or any good melting cheese

Egg Wash (optional)

1 egg (1.75 oz / 50 g)

2 tablespoons water

Position 2 racks in the center of the oven. Preheat the oven to 300°F (149°C). Line 2 baking sheets with parchment paper or silicone mats, then lightly mist the surfaces with spray oil.

In a medium bowl, combine the sesame seed flour, almond flour, baking powder, salt, onion powder, and black pepper and whisk until well mixed. In a large bowl, whisk the eggs. Add the flour mixture and cheese and stir with a large spoon until all of the ingredients are thoroughly combined. The dough will be stiff. Scrape down the sides of the bowl and form the dough into a ball; if it's too dry to form a ball, stir in a bit of water, 1 teaspoon at a time, just until the dough comes together and all of the loose flour is incorporated to make a stiff, playdough-like dough (see page 27).

Mist 2 pieces of parchment paper or 2 silicone mats with spray oil. Place the dough between the oiled surfaces, then use a rolling pin to roll and flatten the dough until slightly thinner than ¼ inch.

Put a bit of vegetable oil in a saucer or small, shallow dish. Dip a 2-inch round biscuit cutter into the oil to coat the cutting edge. Gently peel back the top piece of parchment or silicone mat and cut the crackers.

Peel the cut pieces off the parchment with either your hands or a small metal spatula and transfer them to the prepared pans. They won't spread, so you can position them quite close to each other, nearly touching. Gather any scraps, roll them out, and cut more crackers until all of the dough has been used.

Bake for 12 minutes, then rotate the pans and switch racks and bake for 12 to 15 minutes, until the crackers are golden brown and crisp. Thicker crackers may require longer baking.

Immediately transfer the crackers to a wire rack to cool completely. They will get crispier as they cool.

Cheddar Cheese and Pecan Crackers

MAKES 36 TWO-INCH ROUND CRACKERS

Denene's neighbor said she would drive to the store every single day to buy these crackers. Enough said.

1¹⁄₂ cups (6 oz / 170 g) pecan flour (see page 85)

¹⁄₂ cup (2 oz / 57 g) almond flour

1 cup (4 oz / 113 g) shredded or grated Cheddar cheese

1 teaspoon baking powder

1 teaspoon salt

1 teaspoon dried parsley

¹⁄₂ teaspoon ground black pepper

2 eggs (3.5 oz / 99 g)

Egg Wash (optional)

1 egg (1.75 oz / 50 g)

2 tablespoons water

Position 2 racks in the center of the oven. Preheat the oven to 300°F (149°C). Cover 2 baking sheets with parchment paper or silicone mats, then lightly mist the surfaces with spray oil.

In a medium bowl, combine the pecan flour, almond flour, cheese, baking powder, salt, parsley, and pepper and whisk until well mixed. In a large bowl, whisk the eggs, then add the flour mixture and stir with a large spoon until all of the ingredients are thoroughly combined. The dough will be stiff. Scrape down the sides of the bowl and form the dough into a ball; if it's too dry to form a ball, stir in a bit of water, 1 teaspoon at a time, just until the dough comes together and all of the loose flour is incorporated to make a stiff, playdough-like dough (see page 27).

Mist 2 pieces of parchment paper or 2 silicone mats with spray oil. Place the dough between the oiled surfaces, then use a rolling pin to roll and flatten the dough until slightly thinner than ¼ inch.

Put a bit of vegetable oil in a saucer or small, shallow dish. Dip a 2-inch round biscuit cutter into the oil to coat the cutting edge. Gently peel back the top piece of parchment or silicone mat and cut the crackers.

Peel the cut pieces off the parchment with either your hands or a small metal spatula and transfer them to the prepared pans. They won't spread, so you can position them quite close to each other, nearly touching. Gather any scraps, roll them out, and cut more crackers until all of the dough has been used.

Bake for 12 minutes, then rotate the pans and switch racks and bake for 12 to 15 minutes, until the crackers are golden brown and crisp. Thicker crackers may require longer baking.

Immediately transfer the crackers to a wire rack to cool completely. They will get crispier as they cool.

VARIATIONS

Spicy Cheddar-Pecan Crackers: For a spicier cracker, add ½ teaspoon cayenne pepper when mixing the dry ingredients.

Extra Nutty Crackers: Or, to add even more nut flavor, place a sprinkle of finely chopped pecans on the top of each cracker before baking. During the baking process the pecans will toast up nice and crunchy.

Sesame Seed Breadsticks

MAKES 9 TO 12 BREADSTICKS

Here's a recipe for a basic, simple breadstick that's amenable to endless variations. We've included a few ideas in the sidebar on page 104 to get you started.

2 cups (8 oz / 227 g) almond flour

1 cup (4 oz / 113 g) sesame seed flour

1 1/2 teaspoons baking powder

1/2 teaspoon salt

1/4 teaspoon xanthan gum

2 eggs (3.5 oz / 99 g)

2 tablespoons unsweetened soy milk or other milk

Egg Wash

1 egg (1.75 oz / 50 g)

2 tablespoons water

Toppings

1/2 teaspoon Maldon salt, coarse sea salt, or kosher salt

1 teaspoon sesame seeds

Preheat the oven to 375°F (191°C). Line a baking sheet with parchment paper or a silicone mat.

In a medium bowl, combine the almond flour, sesame seed flour, baking powder, salt, and xanthan gum and whisk until well mixed. In a large bowl, whisk the eggs and milk together until thoroughly blended. Add the dry ingredients and stir with a large spoon for 1 to 2 minutes to make a stiff, playdough-like dough (see page 27).

Mist a work surface with spray oil and transfer the dough to the oiled spot. Divide the dough into 9 to 12 equal portions. Mist your hands with spray oil, then gently roll out each piece of dough to form a breadstick 6 to 8 inches long and about 1/2 inch thick. Place the breadsticks on the prepared pan as you go. They won't spread, so you can position them fairly close to each other.

Make the egg wash by whisking the egg and water together until frothy, then brush the mixture over the breadsticks. Sprinkle the coarse salt evenly over the breadsticks, then do the same with the sesame seeds.

Bake for 15 minutes, then lower the oven temperature to 350°F (177°C), rotate the pan, and bake for about 15 more minutes, until golden brown and firm to the touch.

Immediately transfer the breadsticks to a wire rack and let cool for at least 10 minutes before serving.

Breadstick Variations

Here are a few ideas for creating your own variations on any of the breadstick recipes in this chapter:

- Use different types of nut and seed flours in different proportions. Any combination is fine, as long as the total amount is equal to what's called for in the recipe.

- For softer, cheesy breadsticks, add 1 cup (4 oz / 227 g) of shredded or grated mozzarella, Cheddar, or Swiss cheese when mixing the dry ingredients.

- For sweeter breadsticks, add $1/2$ teaspoon of liquid stevia when mixing the wet ingredients and omit the salt garnish.

- For herbed breadsticks, add 1 teaspoon of dried thyme, herbes de Provence, or minced fresh rosemary when mixing the dry ingredients.

- To make mini breadsticks (sort of like pretzel nuggets), cut each breadstick into three or four smaller pieces after you apply the egg wash and any toppings.

Spicy Breadsticks

MAKES 9 TO 12 BREADSTICKS

These nutty, spicy breadsticks are delicious with any sugar-free jelly, but especially with hot pepper jelly.

2 cups (8 oz / 227 g) almond flour

1/2 cup (2 oz / 57 g) sesame seed flour

1/2 cup (2 oz / 57 g) pecan flour (see page 85)

1 1/2 teaspoons baking powder

1/2 teaspoon salt

1/4 teaspoon xanthan gum

1/2 to 1 teaspoon cayenne pepper

2 eggs (3.5 oz / 99 g)

2 tablespoons unsweetened soy milk or other milk

Egg Wash

1 egg (1.75 oz / 50 g)

2 tablespoons water

Toppings

1/2 teaspoon Maldon salt or coarsely ground sea salt

1 teaspoon sesame seeds

Preheat the oven to 375°F (191°C). Line a baking sheet with parchment paper or a silicone mat.

In a medium bowl, combine the almond flour, sesame seed flour, pecan flour, baking powder, salt, xanthan gum, and cayenne and whisk until well mixed. In a large bowl, whisk the eggs and milk together until thoroughly blended. Add the dry ingredients and stir with a large spoon for 1 to 2 minutes to make a stiff, playdough-like dough (see page 27).

Mist a work surface with spray oil and transfer the dough to the oiled spot. Divide the dough into 9 to 12 equal portions. Mist your hands with spray oil, then gently roll out each piece of dough to form a breadstick 6 to 8 inches long and about ½ inch thick. Place the breadsticks on the prepared pan as you go. They won't spread, so you can position them quite close to each other.

Make the egg wash by whisking the egg and water together until frothy, then brush the mixture over the breadsticks. Sprinkle the sea salt and sesame seeds over the breadsticks.

Bake for 15 minutes, then lower the oven temperature to 350°F (177°C), rotate the pan, and bake for about 15 more minutes, until golden brown and firm to the touch.

Immediately transfer the breadsticks to a wire rack and let cool for at least 10 minutes before serving.

Garlic Breadsticks

MAKES 9 TO 12 BREADSTICKS

These breadsticks are for garlic lovers like us. They are especially useful for dipping into marinara sauce or herbed olive oil, but they also make great snacks.

2 cups (8 oz / 227 g) almond flour

1/2 cup (2 oz / 57 g) sesame seed flour

1/2 cup (2 oz / 57 g) pumpkin seed flour or golden flaxseed meal

1 1/2 teaspoons baking powder

1/2 teaspoon salt

1/4 teaspoon xanthan gum

1 teaspoon garlic powder or granulated garlic, or 1 tablespoon minced fresh garlic

2 eggs (3.5 oz / 99 g)

2 tablespoons unsweetened soy milk or other milk

Egg Wash

1 egg (1.75 oz / 50 g)

2 tablespoons water

Toppings

1/2 teaspoon Maldon salt, coarse sea salt, or garlic salt (optional)

1 teaspoon sesame seeds (optional)

Preheat the oven to 375°F (191°C). Line a baking sheet with parchment paper or a silicone mat.

In a medium bowl, combine the almond flour, sesame seed flour, pumpkin seed flour, baking powder, salt, xanthan gum, and garlic powder and whisk until well mixed. In a large bowl, whisk the eggs and milk together until thoroughly blended. Add the dry ingredients and stir with a large spoon for 1 to 2 minutes to make a stiff, playdough-like dough (see page 27).

Mist a work surface with spray oil and transfer the dough to the oiled spot. Divide the dough into 9 to 12 equal portions. Mist your hands with spray oil, then gently roll out each piece of dough to form a breadstick 6 to 8 inches long and about 1/2 inch thick. Place the breadsticks on the prepared pan as you go. They won't spread, so you can position them quite close to each other.

Make the egg wash by whisking the egg and water together until frothy, then brush the mixture over the breadsticks. Sprinkle the salt and sesame seeds evenly over the breadsticks.

Bake for 15 minutes, then lower the oven temperature to 350°F (177°C), rotate the pan, and bake for about 15 more minutes, until golden brown and firm to the touch.

Immediately transfer the breadsticks to a wire rack and let cool for at least 10 minutes before serving.

Onion Breadsticks

MAKES 9 TO 12 BREADSTICKS

Aside from the various flavor options that each of the seeds offer, the onions provide a sweet and savory flavor note.

2^1/$_2$ cups (10 oz / 283 g) almond flour

^{1}/$_2$ cup (2 oz / 57 g) sesame seed, sunflower seed, or pumpkin seed flour, or a combination

1^1/$_2$ teaspoons baking powder

^{1}/$_2$ teaspoon salt

^{1}/$_4$ teaspoon xanthan gum

^{1}/$_2$ teaspoon onion powder, or 1 tablespoon dried onion flakes

2 eggs (3.5 oz / 99 g)

2 tablespoons unsweetened soy milk or other milk

Egg Wash

1 egg (1.75 oz / 50 g)

2 tablespoons water

Preheat the oven to 375°F (191°C). Line a baking sheet with parchment paper or a silicone mat.

In a medium bowl, combine the almond flour, sesame seed flour, baking powder, salt, xanthan gum, and onion powder and whisk until well mixed. In a large bowl, whisk the eggs and milk together until thoroughly blended. Add the dry ingredients and stir with a large spoon for 1 to 2 minutes to make a stiff, playdough-like dough (see page 27).

Mist a work surface with spray oil and transfer the dough to the oiled spot. Divide the dough into 9 to 12 equal portions. Mist your hands with spray oil, then gently roll out each piece of dough to form a breadstick 6 to 8 inches long and about ½ inch thick. Place the breadsticks on the prepared pan as you go. They won't spread, so you can position them quite close to each other.

Make the egg wash by whisking the egg and water together until frothy, then brush the mixture over the breadsticks.

Bake for 15 minutes, then lower the oven temperature to 350°F (177°C), rotate the pan, and bake for about 15 more minutes, until golden brown and firm to the touch.

Immediately transfer the breadsticks to a wire rack and let cool for at least 10 minutes before serving.

Simple Pretzels

MAKES 8 TO 12 PRETZELS

It simply isn't possible to create a gluten-free, sugar-free pretzel that replicates the texture and flavor of an authentic soft pretzel, especially one dipped in lye, as is done in Pennsylvania Dutch country. Fortunately, it isn't difficult to make a gluten-free, sugar-free pretzel that tastes fantastic. Plus, our version is made with baking soda, a safe, optional alternative to lye that provides a similar alkaline tone that we associate with pretzels. These are delicious with mustard (the "proper" way, as those of us from Philly say). The butter sprinkles are an unusual but essential flavoring ingredient; you can find them near the spices at almost any supermarket. Pretzel salt is available at many stores as well, but you can also use coarse sea salt or kosher salt.

2 cups (8 oz / 227 g) almond flour

1/2 cup (2 oz / 57 g) sunflower seed flour

1/2 cup (2 oz / 57 g) sesame seed flour

2 teaspoons butter-flavored sprinkles

1 1/2 teaspoons baking powder

1/4 teaspoon xanthan gum

1/4 teaspoon salt

2 eggs (3.5 oz / 99 g)

2 1/4 teaspoons (1 package) instant or active dry yeast

2 tablespoons warm water (about 95°F, or 35°C)

Egg Wash

1 egg

1 tablespoon water

1/4 teaspoon baking soda (optional)

Toppings

1/2 to 1 teaspoon Maldon salt, coarse salt, or pretzel salt

1 tablespoon sesame seeds (optional)

Preheat the oven to 350°F (177°C), or for crispier pretzels, preheat the oven to 375°F (191°C). Line a baking sheet with parchment paper or a silicone mat, then lightly mist the surface with spray oil.

In a medium bowl, combine the almond flour, sunflower seed flour, sesame seed flour, butter-flavored sprinkles, baking powder, xanthan gum, and salt and whisk until well mixed. In a large bowl, whisk the eggs. In a small bowl, stir the yeast and water together until the yeast dissolves, then stir the mixture into the eggs (no need to wait for the yeast to bubble, because it's only for flavor, not leavening).

Add the flour mixture to the eggs and stir with a large spoon for 1 to 2 minutes to make a thick, playdough-like dough (see page 27).

Mist a work surface with spray oil and transfer the dough to the oiled spot. Divide the dough into 8 to 12 equal portions and form each into a ball. (You may want to oil your hands to prevent sticking.) Gently roll each ball into a strand 10 to 15 inches long and ½ inch in diameter. If the strands split or fall apart, press them back together; if they're too crumbly to hold together, put the dough back in the bowl and stir in 1 or 2 teaspoons of water. Form each strand into a pretzel shape as shown on page 113, then place the pretzels on the prepared pan. They won't spread, so you can position them fairly close together.

Make the egg wash by whisking the egg, water, and baking soda together until frothy, then brush the mixture over the pretzels. Sprinkle the coarse salt evenly over the pretzels, then do the same with the sesame seeds.

Bake for 12 minutes, then rotate and bake for 12 to 18 minutes, until firm to the touch and golden brown.

Immediately transfer the pretzels to a wire rack using a metal or plastic spatula. Let cool for at least 10 minutes before serving.

Three-Pepper Pretzels

MAKES 8 TO 12 PRETZELS

These spicy pretzels are great with mustard on top. But better yet, try them with salsa or a melted cheese dip! Adjust the amounts of cayenne and pepper to suit your palate.

3 cups (12 oz / 340 g) almond flour

2 teaspoons butter-flavored sprinkles

1 1/2 teaspoons baking powder

1/4 teaspoon xanthan gum

1/4 teaspoon salt

1 teaspoon crushed red pepper flakes

1/2 to 1 teaspoon cayenne pepper

1/4 to 3/4 teaspoon ground black or white pepper

2 eggs (3.5 oz / 99 g)

2 1/4 teaspoons (1 package) instant or active dry yeast

2 tablespoons warm water (about 95°F, or 35°C)

Egg Wash

1 egg

1 tablespoon water

1/4 teaspoon baking soda

Toppings

1/2 to 1 teaspoon Maldon salt, coarse salt, or pretzel salt (optional)

1 tablespoon sesame seeds (optional)

Preheat the oven to 350°F (177°C), or for crispier pretzels, preheat the oven to 375°F (191°C). Line a baking sheet with parchment paper or a silicone mat, then lightly mist the surface with spray oil.

In a medium bowl, combine the almond flour, butter-flavored sprinkles, baking powder, xanthan gum, salt, red pepper flakes, cayenne, and black pepper and whisk until well mixed. In a large bowl, whisk the eggs. In a small bowl, stir the yeast and water together until the yeast dissolves, then stir the mixture into the eggs (no need to wait for the yeast to bubble, because it's only for flavor, not leavening).

Add the flour mixture to the eggs and stir with a large spoon for 1 to 2 minutes to make a stiff, playdough-like dough (see page 27).

Mist a work surface with spray oil and transfer the dough to the oiled spot. Divide the dough into 8 to 12 equal portions and form each into a ball. (You may want to oil your hands to prevent sticking.) Gently roll each ball into a strand 10 to 15 inches long and ½ inch in diameter. If the strands split or fall apart, press them back together; if they're too crumbly to hold together, put the dough back in the bowl and stir in 1 or 2 teaspoons of water. Form each strand into a pretzel shape as shown opposite, then place the pretzels on the prepared pan. They won't spread, so you can position them fairly close together.   (CONTINUED)

Make the egg wash by whisking the egg, water, and baking soda together until frothy, then brush the mixture over the pretzels. Sprinkle the coarse salt evenly over the pretzels, then do the same with the sesame seeds.

Bake for 12 minutes, then rotate and bake for 12 to 18 minutes, until firm to the touch and golden brown.

Immediately transfer the pretzels to a wire rack using a metal or plastic spatula. Let cool for at least 10 minutes before serving.

Shaping Pretzels

There is no longer one correct way to shape a pretzel. The classic "Holy Trinity" shape created in monasteries centuries ago to feed hungry pilgrims has now given way to pretzel sticks, nubs, and any number of curvy shapes, and pretzels are sold in both crisp and soft styles. Our recipes produce crisp-style pretzels, and they can be made in any shape you like. The photos offer a few examples, but the main thing to know is that you should apply gentle but firm pressure to extrude the dough into a length that can then be gently curved or bent. Rub a small amount of vegetable oil onto your work surface (just a light coating) to facilitate the process and to keep the dough from sticking. Work with the dough slowly until you master your own method, but don't worry if the dough splits or breaks as you shape it—you can always press or squeeze it back into shape. If the dough crumbles, use wet fingers to paste it back together. It won't take long for you to master the shaping and, once you do, you can make pretzels in any shape and size.

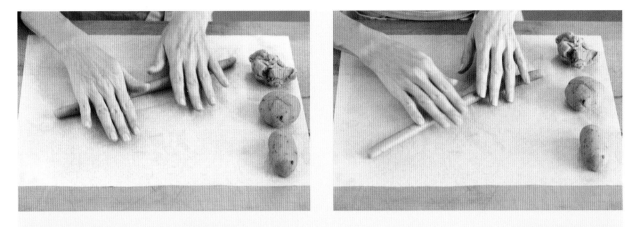

Onion Pretzels

We love the onion flavor in these pretzels in combination with the sesame seed flour, and it's really hard to stop eating them once you get going.

2¹/₂ cups (10 oz / 283 g) almond flour

¹/₂ cup (2 oz / 57 g) sesame seed flour

2 teaspoons butter-flavored sprinkles

1¹/₂ teaspoons baking powder

¹/₄ teaspoon xanthan gum

¹/₄ teaspoon salt

2 teaspoons onion powder, or 4 tablespoons dried onion flakes

2 eggs (3.5 oz / 99 g)

2¹/₄ teaspoons (1 package) instant or active dry yeast

2 tablespoons warm water (about 95°F, or 35°C)

Egg Wash

1 egg

1 tablespoon water

¹/₄ teaspoon baking soda

Toppings

¹/₂ to 1 teaspoon coarse salt or pretzel salt (optional)

1 tablespoon sesame seeds (optional)

Preheat the oven to 350°F (177°C), or for crispier pretzels, preheat the oven to 375°F (191°C). Line a baking sheet with parchment paper or a silicone mat, then lightly mist the surface with spray oil.

In a medium bowl, combine the almond flour, sesame seed flour, butter-flavored sprinkles, baking powder, xanthan gum, salt, and onion powder and whisk until well mixed. In a large bowl, whisk the eggs. In a small bowl, stir the yeast and water together until the yeast dissolves, then stir the mixture into the eggs (no need to wait for the yeast to bubble, because it's only for flavor, not leavening).

Add the flour mixture to the eggs and stir with a large spoon for 1 to 2 minutes to make a stiff, playdough-like dough (see page 27).

Mist a work surface with spray oil and transfer the dough to the oiled spot. Divide the dough into 8 to 12 equal portions and form each into a ball. (You may want to oil your hands to prevent sticking.) Gently roll each ball into a strand 10 to 15 inches long and ½ inch in diameter. If the strands split or fall apart, press them back together; if they're too crumbly to hold together, put the dough back in the bowl and stir in 1 or 2 teaspoons of water. Form each strand into a pretzel shape as shown on page 113, then place the pretzels on the prepared pan. They won't spread, so you can position them fairly close together.

Make the egg wash by whisking the egg, water, and baking soda together until frothy, then brush the mixture over the pretzels. Sprinkle the coarse salt evenly over the pretzels, then do the same with the sesame seeds.

Bake for 12 minutes, then rotate and bake for 12 to 18 minutes, until firm to the touch and golden brown.

Immediately transfer the pretzels to a wire rack using a metal or plastic spatula. Let cool for at least 10 minutes before serving.

Garlic Pretzels

MAKES 8 TO 12 PRETZELS

Garlic is probably the most popular add-in for pretzels, whether in the dough or on top. We prefer to mix it in the dough, leaving plenty of space for salt or sesame seeds on the top. Regardless, these are for those who are not afraid of a little garlic breath.

2 cups (8 oz / 227 g) almond flour

1/2 cup (2 oz / 57 g) pecan or walnut flour (see page 85)

1/2 cup (2 oz / 57 g) sesame seed flour

2 teaspoons butter-flavored sprinkles

1 1/2 teaspoons baking powder

1/4 teaspoon xanthan gum

1/4 teaspoon salt

1 tablespoon minced fresh garlic, or 1 1/2 teaspoons granulated garlic

2 eggs (3.5 oz / 99 g)

2 1/4 teaspoons (1 package) instant or active dry yeast

2 tablespoons warm water (about 95°F, or 35°C)

Egg Wash

1 egg

1 tablespoon water

1/4 teaspoon baking soda

Toppings

1/2 to 1 teaspoon coarse salt or pretzel salt (optional)

1 tablespoon sesame seeds (optional)

Preheat the oven to 350°F (177°C), or for crisper pretzels, preheat the oven to 375°F (191°C). Line a baking sheet with parchment paper or a silicone mat, then lightly mist the surface with spray oil.

In a medium bowl, combine the almond flour, pecan flour, sesame seed flour, butter-flavored sprinkles, baking powder, xanthan gum, salt, and garlic and whisk until well mixed. In a large bowl, whisk the eggs. In a small bowl, stir the yeast and water together until the yeast dissolves, then stir the mixture into the eggs (no need to wait for the yeast to bubble, because it's only for flavor, not leavening).

Add the flour mixture to the eggs and stir with a large spoon for 1 to 2 minutes to make a stiff, playdough-like dough (see page 27).

Mist a work surface with spray oil and transfer the dough to the oiled spot. Divide the dough into 8 to 12 equal portions and form each into a ball. (You may want to oil your hands to prevent sticking.) Gently roll each ball into a strand 10 to 15 inches long and ½ inch in diameter. If the strands split or fall apart, press them back together; if they're too crumbly to hold together, put the dough back in the bowl and stir in 1 or 2 teaspoons of water. Form each strand into a pretzel shape as shown on page 113, then place the pretzels on the prepared pan. They won't spread, so you can position them fairly close together.

Make the egg wash by whisking the egg, water, and baking soda together until frothy, then brush the mixture over the pretzels. Sprinkle the coarse salt evenly over the pretzels, then do the same with the sesame seeds.

Bake for 12 minutes, then rotate and bake for 12 to 18 minutes, until firm to the touch and golden brown.

Immediately transfer the pretzels to a wire rack using a metal or plastic spatula. Let cool for at least 10 minutes before serving.

Chapter Four

MUFFINS, SCONES, PANCAKES, WAFFLES, AND OTHER BREAKFAST TREATS

Many of the recipes in this book can serve as breakfast treats. However, some baked goods, such as muffins and scones, are typically thought of as morning treats, so we've gathered them in this chapter, along with pancakes, waffles, quick breads (which are, essentially, loaf versions of a muffin), and even a sweet biscuit recipe. But turnabout is fair play, and these delicious creations shouldn't be limited to morning fare. Enjoy them as a healthful snack whenever you want! As with all of the recipes in this book, feel free to experiment with different nut and seed flours and different ratios of flours.

Here are a few tips to help ensure success when making breakfast pastries:

- When making the muffin recipes, be sure to line the muffin cups with paper or foil liners or simply coat the muffin tins with a generous amount of butter-flavored spray oil. These muffins tend to be sticky, so if you don't use liners, you may have trouble getting them out of the pan in one piece.

- When making larger batches of muffins or scones, you'll have the best results if you bake just one pan at a time. You have the option of baking the second pan after the first one comes out of the oven or chilling the dough and baking the muffins or scones at a later time. If you do bake them later, note that chilled dough may take longer to bake; if time permits, give the batter an hour or so at room temperature to take off the chill.

- The scones in this chapter have excellent flavor and texture. If you prefer thicker scones, bake them in muffin pans or mini muffin pans, generously misted with spray oil.

- Feel free to make the scones larger or smaller than we specify, but note that you'll need to adjust the baking time accordingly. Smaller scones will bake more quickly, and larger scones will take longer.

- Pancakes and waffles should, of course, be served hot off the griddle (or waffle iron). The muffins, scones, and other baked goods in this chapter can be served warm, at room temperature, or cold.

- Store leftover breakfast pastries in the refrigerator for up to two weeks or in the freezer for up to three months in airtight containers or resealable bags, with a paper towel beneath them to absorb oil.

Blueberry-Hazelnut Muffins

MAKES 9 MUFFINS

Hazelnut flour takes these muffins in a delectable direction. And given that both hazelnuts and blueberries thrive in the Pacific Northwest, it comes as no surprise that their flavors have a natural affinity. That said, you can certainly substitute almond or other nut flours for some or all of the hazelnut flour.

3/4 cup (3 oz / 85 g) hazelnut flour

3/4 cup (3 oz / 85 g) almond flour

1/2 cup Splenda or Stevia Extract in the Raw, or 1/4 cup New Roots Stevia Sugar

1/3 cup (about 1.65 oz / 47 g) almonds or hazelnuts, chopped

1 tablespoon baking powder

1/4 teaspoon salt

2 eggs (3.5 oz / 99 g)

1/2 cup (4 oz / 113 g) unsweetened soy milk or other milk

1 1/2 teaspoons vanilla extract

1 teaspoon fresh lemon juice

1/2 teaspoon liquid stevia

1/2 to 1 cup (2.5 to 5 oz / 71 to 142 g) fresh or frozen blueberries, depending on dietary restrictions

Preheat the oven to 350°F (177°C). Line 9 muffin cups with paper or foil liners, then lightly mist them with spray oil (or omit the liners and generously mist the muffin cups with spray oil).

In a medium bowl, combine the hazelnut flour, almond flour, Splenda, almonds, baking powder, and salt and whisk until well mixed. In a large bowl, whisk the eggs, milk, vanilla, lemon juice, and liquid stevia together until thoroughly blended. Add the flour mixture and stir with a large spoon for 1 to 2 minutes to make a smooth, sticky batter (see page 27). Gently fold in the blueberries.

Spoon or scoop the batter into the prepared muffin cups, dividing it evenly among them; the muffin cups should be just about full.

Bake for 20 minutes, then rotate and bake for 20 more minutes, until golden brown and firm and springy when pressed in the center.

Let the muffins cool in the pan for at least 10 minutes before turning them out onto a wire rack.

VARIATION

Blueberry Crumb Muffins: Before mixing the batter, prepare the crumb topping as directed on page 189. After portioning the batter into the pan, sprinkle the topping evenly over the muffins, then bake as described above.

Almond, Hazelnut, and Raspberry Muffins

MAKES 12 MUFFINS

Although this recipe calls for raspberries, you can use any type of berry for these delightful muffins.

1¹/₂ cups (6 oz / 170 g) almond flour

1¹/₂ cups (6 oz / 170 g) hazelnut flour

¹/₂ cup Splenda or Stevia Extract in the Raw, or ¹/₄ cup New Roots Stevia Sugar

4 teaspoons baking powder

4 eggs (7 oz / 198 g)

¹/₂ cup (4 oz / 113 g) unsweetened soy milk or other milk

2 tablespoons vanilla extract

¹/₄ teaspoon liquid stevia

1¹/₂ cups (about 6.5 oz / 184 g) fresh or frozen unsweetened raspberries, or more, depending on dietary restrictions (but no more than 2 cups)

Preheat the oven to 350°F (177°C). Line 12 muffin cups with paper or foil liners, then mist them with spray oil (or omit the liners and mist the muffin cups generously with spray oil).

In a medium bowl, combine the almond flour, hazelnut flour, Splenda, and baking powder and whisk until well mixed. In a large bowl, whisk the eggs, milk, vanilla, and liquid stevia together until thoroughly blended. Add the flour mixture and stir with a large spoon for 1 to 2 minutes to make a smooth, sticky batter (see page 27). Gently fold in the raspberries.

Spoon or scoop the batter into the prepared muffin cups, dividing it evenly among them; the muffin cups should be just about full.

Bake for 15 minutes, then rotate and bake for 15 to 20 more minutes, until firm and springy when pressed in the center.

Let the muffins cool in the pan for at least 15 minutes before turning them out onto a wire rack.

VARIATION

Raspberry Crumb Muffins: Before mixing the batter, prepare the crumb topping as directed on page 189. After portioning the batter into the pan, sprinkle the topping evenly over the muffins, then bake as described above.

Strawberry-Coconut Muffins

MAKES 12 MUFFINS

The key to this recipe is the generous amount of coconut flour and shredded coconut. In combination with juicy, tangy fruit, it evokes a summer day on a warm tropical island. Below the recipe, we've suggested a couple of variations on the theme using fruit other than strawberries, but don't let those limit your thinking. You can use any kind of berries, and almost any fresh fruit, in these tender, moist muffins.

1 cup (4 oz / 113 g) almond flour

1/2 cup (2 oz / 57 g) coconut flour (see Tip, page 14)

1/2 cup (1.5 oz / 43 g) unsweetened shredded dried coconut, lightly toasted (see Tip, page 150)

1 cup Splenda or Stevia Extract in the Raw, or 1/2 cup New Roots Stevia Sugar

4 teaspoons baking powder

4 eggs (7 oz / 198 g)

1 1/2 cups (12 oz / 340 g) unsweetened soy milk or other milk

2 teaspoons vanilla extract

2 teaspoons fresh lemon juice

1 1/4 teaspoons liquid stevia

1 cup (5.25 oz / 149 g) fresh or frozen unsweetened strawberries, sliced or coarsely chopped

Preheat the oven to 350°F (177°C). Line 12 muffin cups with paper or foil liners, then lightly mist them with spray oil (or omit the liners and mist the muffin cups generously with spray oil).

In a medium bowl, combine the almond flour, coconut flour, shredded coconut, Splenda, and baking powder and whisk until well mixed. In a large bowl, whisk the eggs, milk, vanilla, lemon juice, and liquid stevia together until thoroughly blended. Add the flour mixture and stir with a large spoon for 1 to 2 minutes to make a smooth, sticky batter (see page 27). Gently fold in the strawberries.

Scoop or spoon the batter into the prepared muffin cups, dividing it evenly among them; the muffin cups should be just about full.

Bake for 20 minutes, then rotate and bake for 20 to 25 more minutes, until golden brown and springy when pressed in the center.

Let the muffins cool in the pan for at least 10 minutes before turning them out onto a wire rack.

VARIATIONS

Mango Muffins: Substitute chopped fresh or frozen mango (not canned) for the strawberries.

Piña Colada Muffins: Use chopped fresh pineapple (not canned) in place of the strawberries.

Cinnamon-Apple Muffins

MAKES 9 MUFFINS

These muffins, which feature the classic cinnamon-apple flavor synergy, taste like homemade apple pie, but without the hassle of making piecrust. If you're sensitive to the sugars in fruits, Granny Smith, pippin, or another tart apple is your best bet. Another advantage to Granny Smith and pippin apples is that they're firm and have more texture when baked. However, any apple will work just fine in this recipe. We recommend leaving the skin on, since it contributes fiber, but again, it's your call; feel free to peel the apple if you like.

3/4 cup (3 oz / 85 g) hazelnut flour

3/4 cup (3 oz / 85 g) almond flour

1/2 cup Splenda or Stevia Extract in the Raw, or 1/4 cup New Roots Stevia Sugar

1 tablespoon baking powder

1 teaspoon ground cinnamon

2 eggs (3.5 oz / 99 g)

6 tablespoons (3 oz / 85 g) unsweetened soy milk or other milk

2 tablespoons unsweetened applesauce

1 1/2 teaspoons vanilla extract

1/2 teaspoon liquid stevia

1/2 cup (4.5 oz / 128 g) coarsely chopped apple (about 1 large apple)

1/4 cup (1 oz / 28 g) chopped almonds, pecans, hazelnuts, or walnuts, for garnish

Preheat the oven to 350°F (177°C). Line 9 muffin cups with paper or foil liners, then mist them with spray oil (or omit the liners and mist the muffin cups generously with spray oil).

In a medium bowl, combine the hazelnut flour, almond flour, Splenda, baking powder, and cinnamon and whisk until well mixed. In a large bowl whisk the eggs, milk, applesauce, vanilla, and liquid stevia together until thoroughly blended. Add the flour mixture and stir with a large spoon for 1 to 2 minutes to make a smooth, sticky batter (see page 27). Fold in the apples.

Spoon or scoop the batter into the prepared muffin cups, dividing it evenly among them; the muffin cups should be just about full. Sprinkle the nuts evenly over the muffins.

Bake for 20 minutes, then rotate and bake for about 20 to 25 more minutes, until golden brown and springy when pressed in the center.

Let the muffins cool in the pan for at least 5 minutes before turning them out onto a wire rack.

Cranberry Scones

MAKES 20 TO 24 SCONES

Delightfully aromatic while evoking the holiday season, this scone recipe will please everyone. The only sugars are from the cranberries and cranberry juice, but they are amply balanced by the nut fiber. Although these scones are gluten-free and low in carbs, they capture the essence of a good scone: moist and not dry.

3 cups (12 oz / 340 g) almond flour

2 cups (8 oz / 227 g) pecan flour (see page 12)

1¼ cups Splenda or Stevia Extract in the Raw, or ½ cup plus 2 tablespoons New Roots Stevia Sugar

1½ teaspoons baking powder

½ teaspoon salt

1 teaspoon ground cinnamon

½ teaspoon ground cloves

3 eggs (5.25 oz / 149 g)

½ cup (4 oz / 113 g) unsweetened cranberry juice

¼ cup (2 oz / 57 g) salted butter or margarine, melted

½ teaspoon liquid stevia

¼ to 1 cup (1.25 to 5 oz / 35 to 142 g) dried cranberries, raisins, or a combination; the amount depends on dietary restrictions

Position 2 oven racks in the middle of the oven. Preheat the oven to 350°F (177°C). Line 2 baking sheets with parchment paper or silicone mats or mist them with spray oil.

In a medium bowl, combine the almond flour, pecan flour, Splenda, baking powder, salt, cinnamon, and cloves and whisk until well mixed. In a large bowl, whisk the eggs, juice, butter, and liquid stevia together until thoroughly blended. Add the flour mixture and stir with a large spoon for about 1 minute to make a thick, sticky batter that will hold its shape when dropped from a spoon (see page 27). Add the dried cranberries and stir just until the fruit is evenly distributed.

Drop the batter onto the prepared pans, using 2 heaping tablespoons of batter per scone and spacing them about 2 inches apart.

Bake for 12 minutes, then rotate the pans and switch racks and bake for about 10 minutes, until the scones are light brown and firm to the touch. (You can also bake one pan at a time or save some of the dough for another time.)

Immediately transfer the scones to a wire rack and let cool for about 10 minutes before serving. Serve warm, at room temperature, or cold.

Lemon and Poppy Seed Scones

MAKES 20 TO 24 SCONES

Poppy seeds add such a nice flavor and texture to baked goods, and lemon and poppy seed are a popular flavor combination. This recipe takes advantage of the whole lemon, so feel free to add the lemon pulp along with the juice—consider it a bonus ingredient, adding more lemon flavor and texture. Although we call for almond flour only, these scones are also delicious with a bit of pecan or sunflower seed flour. By the way, these make a delicious accompaniment to anything citrusy—from orange juice to any flavor of fruit sorbet, especially lemon. One caveat: Don't try to substitute vegetable oil for the butter or margarine in this recipe. It just won't create the same flavor synergy with the lemon juice that you'll get from butter or a good-quality buttery spread.

4 cups (1 lb / 454 g) almond flour

1¼ cups Splenda or Stevia Extract in the Raw, or ½ cup plus 2 tablespoons New Roots Stevia Sugar

1½ teaspoons baking powder

¼ teaspoon salt

1 tablespoon poppy seeds

3 eggs (5.25 oz / 149 g)

½ cup (4 oz / 113 g) fresh lemon juice

¼ cup (2 oz / 57 g) salted butter or margarine, melted

3 tablespoons grated lemon zest

2 teaspoons vanilla extract

¼ teaspoon liquid stevia

Position 2 oven racks in the middle of the oven. Preheat the oven to 350°F (177°C). Line 2 baking sheets with parchment paper or silicone mats or lightly mist them with spray oil.

In a medium bowl, combine the almond flour, Splenda, baking powder, salt, and poppy seeds and whisk until well mixed. In a large bowl, whisk the eggs, lemon juice, butter, lemon zest, vanilla, and liquid stevia together until thoroughly blended. Add the flour mixture and stir with a large spoon for 1 to 2 minutes to make a thick, sticky batter that will hold its shape when dropped from a spoon (see page 27).

Drop the batter onto the prepared pans, using 2 heaping tablespoons of batter per scone and spacing them 2 inches apart.

Bake for 10 minutes, then rotate the pans and switch racks and bake for about 10 more minutes, until the scones are golden brown and firm to the touch.

Immediately transfer the scones to a wire rack and let cool for at least 10 minutes before serving. (CONTINUED)

VARIATION

Lemon-Frosted Scones: For added zing and more lemon flavor, make a frosting by whisking ½ cup of Stevia Extract in the Raw, Splenda, Truvia, or ZSweet with the juice of 1 lemon. Spread the frosting over the scones before serving.

Chocolate-Coconut Scones

MAKES 20 TO 24 SCONES

These chocolaty scones are soft and chewy in the center but crisp on the surface. If you prefer scones that are crisp all the way through, simply make them smaller. The coconut adds a wonderful, macaroon-like flavor and texture. We prefer to use Low Carb Specialties ChocoPerfection chocolate bars because they have great melting qualities and minimal carbs; just cut the bars into small bits with a sharp knife. However, you can certainly substitute any brand of sugar-free chocolate chips. Note that this recipe is written to use unsweetened chocolate soy milk or almond milk. If you happen to find a sugar-free sweetened chocolate milk, or if sugar isn't an issue and you use sweetened chocolate milk, omit the liquid stevia.

2 cups (8 oz / 227 g) hazelnut flour

2 cups (8 oz / 227 g) almond flour

1¼ cups Splenda or Stevia Extract in the Raw, or ½ cup plus 2 tablespoons New Roots Stevia Sugar

½ cup (1.5 oz / 43 g) unsweetened shredded dried coconut

½ cup (1.5 oz / 43 g) unsweetened cocoa powder, natural or Dutch-process

1½ teaspoons baking powder

½ teaspoon salt

¼ teaspoon baking soda

3 eggs (5.25 oz / 149 g)

1 cup (8 oz / 227 g) unsweetened chocolate soy milk or almond milk

2 teaspoons vanilla extract

¼ teaspoon liquid stevia

1 cup sugar-free chocolate chips (see page 21)

Position 2 oven racks in the middle of the oven. Preheat the oven to 350°F (177°C). Line 2 baking sheets with parchment paper or silicone mats, or mist them with spray oil.

In a medium bowl, combine the hazelnut flour, almond flour, Splenda, coconut, cocoa powder, baking powder, salt, and baking soda and whisk until well mixed. In a large bowl, whisk the eggs, milk, vanilla extract, and liquid stevia together until thoroughly blended. Add the flour mixture and stir with a large spoon for 1 to 2 minutes to make a thick, sticky batter that will hold its shape when dropped from a spoon (see page 27). Fold in the chocolate chips.

Drop the batter onto the prepared pans, using 2 heaping tablespoons of batter per scone and spacing them 2 inches apart.

Bake for 10 minutes, then rotate and switch racks and bake for about 8 more minutes, until the scones are firm to the touch.

Immediately transfer the scones to a wire rack to cool for at least 10 minutes before serving.

Everyday Pancakes

MAKES 8 TO 10 FOUR- TO SIX-INCH PANCAKES

Sometimes you just want pancakes. This is our basic, all-purpose version, and although you can embellish them with fruit or chopped nuts, why bother when they are so good, especially when slathered with butter or a good-quality buttery spread and sugar-free maple-flavored syrup? This batter will also make wonderful waffles.

1 cup (4 oz / 113 g) hazelnut flour

1 cup (4 oz / 113 g) almond flour

1/4 cup Splenda or Stevia Extract in the Raw, or 2 tablespoons New Roots Stevia Sugar

1 teaspoon baking powder

1/4 teaspoon salt

1 egg (1.75 oz / 50 g)

1/2 cup (4 oz / 113 g) unsweetened soy milk or other milk

1/4 cup (2 oz / 57 g) water

1 teaspoon vanilla extract (optional)

In a medium bowl, combine the hazelnut flour, almond flour, sweetener, baking powder, and salt and whisk until well mixed. In a large bowl, whisk the egg, milk, water, and vanilla together until thoroughly blended. Add the flour mixture and stir with a large spoon or whisk just until all of the ingredients are evenly blended into a loose, pourable batter (see page 27).

Heat a nonstick griddle or skillet over medium heat. When a few drops of water splashed on the surface sizzle and evaporate quickly, the pan is hot enough for cooking pancakes. Mist the pan with spray oil or put about 1 teaspoon of butter or margarine on the pan and swirl to coat the surface.

Portion pancakes onto the pan, using about ¼ cup of batter per pancake and leaving a bit of space between them. The batter should sizzle when it hits the pan. Lower the heat to medium-low and cook the first side for about 4 minutes, until the bottom is golden brown and the top begins to dry out. Flip the pancakes over and cook the second side for 3 to 4 minutes, until the center is springy when pressed. Serve hot.

Tips for Great Pancakes and Waffles

Here are a few tips to help make a festive breakfast even better:

- Be sure to use a nonstick pan or griddle when cooking pancakes. Most waffle irons are nonstick, which is a good thing, because that's what you'll need for these recipes.

- Adequately preheat your pan or waffle iron. Use a measuring cup or ladle to portion even-sized pancakes onto the pan.

- We call for using 1/4 cup of batter per pancake, but you can certainly make your cakes larger or smaller. With waffles, the size is ultimately determined by the size of your waffle iron.

- The key to great pancakes and waffles is patience. Follow the doneness cues in the recipe and don't flip pancakes or try to remove waffles too soon. These pancakes take longer to cook than their conventional counterparts; make sure the underside is medium brown before flipping.

- The heat level is also important. If it's too high, the surface will brown before the interior is adequately cooked. If it's too low, the cakes will take too long to cook and won't develop that appealing crispy exterior. It may take a few tries before you find the best heat level. However, do note that nut flours are oilier than grain-based flours, so the finished pancakes will be moist inside.

- If you'd like to serve all of the pancakes at once, hold the cooked cakes in a warm oven (about 200°F, or 93°C) until you've cooked all the batter.

- Another option when serving a crowd is to make small, silver dollar pancakes. They'll cook more quickly, and the first batch will keep people occupied while you make more.

- For optimum enjoyment, serve slathered with butter or a high-quality buttery spread, and drizzled with sugar-free maple-flavored syrup (or pure maple syrup if sugar isn't an issue for you). We recommend Maple Grove Farms Vermont brand sugar-free maple-flavored syrup, which you can find in most grocery stores alongside all of the other syrups. It has the lowest carb count that we've found and the best flavor!

- You can make a tasty alternative topping by heating sugar-free jam until it thins into a delicious fruit syrup.

Blueberry Pancakes

MAKES 8 TO 10 FOUR- TO SIX-INCH PANCAKES

A great blueberry pancake is the holy grail for most pancake lovers, and these will satisfy even the most picky pancake purist. If you're sensitive to sugar, the balance of ingredients in this recipe will allow you to indulge in blueberries in moderation. And if carbs aren't a concern, feel free to use a full cup of berries. If you use frozen blueberries, leave them in the freezer until just before adding them to the batter. Thawed blueberries will bleed juice into the batter. The pancakes will still taste good, but you'll lose some of the nice color contrast that makes blueberry pancakes visually appealing. Feel free to use this batter to make waffles as well.

1¹/₂ cups (6 oz / 170 g) almond flour

¹/₂ cup (2 oz / 57 g) pecan or walnut flour (see page 12)

¹/₄ cup Splenda or Stevia Extract in the Raw, or 2 tablespoons New Roots Stevia Sugar

1 teaspoon baking powder

¹/₄ teaspoon salt

1 egg (1.75 oz / 50 g)

¹/₂ cup (4 oz / 113 g) unsweetened soy milk or other milk

¹/₄ cup (2 oz / 57 g) water

¹/₂ teaspoon vanilla extract

¹/₄ to 1 cup (1.25 to 5 oz / 35 to 142 g) fresh or frozen, unthawed blueberries, depending on dietary restrictions

In a medium bowl, combine the almond flour, pecan flour, sweetener, baking powder, and salt and whisk until well mixed. In a large bowl, whisk the egg, milk, water, and vanilla until thoroughly blended. Add the flour mixture and stir with a large spoon or whisk just until all of the ingredients are evenly blended into a loose, pourable batter (see page 27). Gently fold in the blueberries.

Heat a nonstick griddle or skillet over medium heat. When a few drops of water splashed on the surface sizzle and evaporate quickly, the pan is hot enough for cooking pancakes. Mist the pan with spray oil or put about 1 teaspoon of butter or margarine on the pan and swirl to coat the surface.

Portion pancakes onto the pan, using about ¼ cup of batter per pancake and leaving a bit of space between them. The batter should sizzle when it hits the pan. Lower the heat to medium-low and cook the first side for about 4 minutes, until the bottom is golden brown and the top begins to dry out. Flip the pancakes over and cook the second side for 3 to 4 minutes, until the center is springy when pressed. Serve hot.

Chocolate Chip Pancakes

MAKES 8 TO 10 FOUR- TO SIX-INCH PANCAKES

These fun pancakes are universally loved by kids and adults alike. You can use any brand of sugar-free chocolate chips for these pancakes. If using ChocoPerfection chocolate bars, chop them into pieces.

2 cups (8 oz / 227 g) almond flour

1/4 cup Splenda or Stevia Extract in the Raw, or 2 tablespoons New Roots Stevia Sugar

1 teaspoon baking powder

1/4 teaspoon salt

1 egg (1.75 oz / 50 g)

1/2 cup (4 oz / 113 g) unsweetened soy milk or other milk

1/4 cup (2 oz / 57 g) water

1 teaspoon vanilla extract

1/2 cup sugar-free chocolate chips (see page 21), or more as desired

In a medium bowl, combine the almond flour, sweetener, baking powder, and salt and whisk until well mixed. In a large bowl, whisk the egg, milk, water, and vanilla together until thoroughly blended. Add the flour mixture and stir with a large spoon just until all of the ingredients are evenly blended into a smooth, pourable batter (see page 27). Fold in the chocolate chips.

Heat a nonstick griddle or skillet over medium heat. When a few drops of water splashed on the surface sizzle and evaporate quickly, the pan is hot enough for cooking pancakes. Mist the pan with spray oil or put about 1 teaspoon of butter or margarine on the pan and swirl to coat the surface.

Portion pancakes onto the pan, using about ¼ cup of batter per pancake and leaving a bit of space between them. The batter should sizzle when it hits the pan. Lower the heat to medium-low and cook the first side for about 4 minutes, until the bottom is golden brown and the top begins to dry out. Flip the pancakes over and cook the second side for 3 to 4 minutes, until the center is springy when pressed. Serve hot.

Waffles

MAKES THREE 6½-INCH ROUND WAFFLES

This recipe is very simple to make. However, it does require an electric mixer (or a strong, vigorous arm and a sturdy whisk) to achieve good aeration. Of course, it also requires a waffle iron, though you could make pancakes with this batter if you thin it with a bit of water. Be sure to spray the waffle iron generously with spray oil, and for optimum flavor, use butter-flavored spray oil. One final note: When making the pecan flour for this recipe, grind it as finely as possible—but not so much that you make nut butter!

1 cup (4 oz / 113 g) pecan flour (see page 12)

1 cup (4 oz / 113 g) almond flour

2 teaspoons baking powder

1/8 teaspoon ground nutmeg

2 eggs (3.5 oz / 99 g)

1/2 cup (4 oz / 113 g) unsweetened soy milk or other milk

1/8 teaspoon liquid stevia (optional)

Preheat a waffle iron; if it has a temperature control, set it to medium-high or high heat.

Put all of the ingredients in a large bowl or the bowl of an electric mixer. Whisk vigorously or mix with the whip attachment at medium speed for about 3 minutes, stopping every minute or so to scrape down the bowl; the batter should be foamy. Whisk even more vigorously or mix at high speed for a few seconds to further aerate the batter. The batter should be loose and pourable (see page 27).

Generously spray both sides of the waffle iron with spray oil. Ladle in enough batter to completely cover the surface once the lid is lowered; the amount will depend on the size of your waffle iron. The batter should sizzle when it contacts the waffle iron.

Cook until the waffle is completely browned and crisp; the amount of time will vary depending on your waffle iron. Repeat with the remaining batter. The batter may stiffen somewhat between making each batch of waffles; if so, add more soy milk to bring the batter back to its original consistency. Serve hot.   (CONTINUED)

WAFFLES, *continued*

VARIATIONS

Pecan Waffles: Substitute more pecan flour for the almond flour.

Banana Waffles: Add ¼ to ½ cup mashed ripe banana when mixing the batter, depending on dietary restrictions. For more banana flavor, add ½ teaspoon banana flavoring or extract.

Blueberry Waffles: Puree ¼ cup of fresh or frozen blueberries and add them when mixing the batter. Ensure the puree is completely smooth so the berries won't stick to the waffle iron.

Sweet Potato, Pecan, and Ginger Biscuits

MAKES 12 TO 15 BISCUITS

Pecans and sweet potatoes—what could be more Southern? Be sure to make these delectable biscuits, and when you do, serve them in the traditional Southern way: slathered with butter or your favorite buttery spread and drizzled with sugar-free maple-flavored syrup. Denene, who was raised in the South, watched her mother press down biscuits with the edge of her hand, as described in the method below. However, you can also press the biscuits with a metal or plastic spatula, leave them as balls, or simply drop them from a spoon for a more rustic shape. One last note, just in case you wonder about sweet potatoes (after all, the name does include "sweet"): Although they do have a wonderful sweet flavor, their carbs are balanced by their natural fiber content.

2 cups (8 oz / 227 g) almond flour

1 cup (4 oz / 113 g) pecan flour (see page 12)

1/2 cup Splenda or Stevia Extract in the Raw, or 1/4 cup New Roots Stevia Sugar

1 1/2 teaspoons baking powder

1/4 teaspoon xanthan gum

1/4 teaspoon salt (optional)

2 1/2 teaspoons ground ginger

1 egg (1.75 oz / 50 g)

1/2 cup (4 oz / 113 g) cooked, mashed sweet potato or yam, at room temperature (see page 140)

1 tablespoon sugar-free maple-flavored syrup

Preheat the oven to 350°F (177°C). Lightly mist a baking pan with spray oil or line it with parchment paper or a silicone mat and then mist the surface.

In a medium bowl, combine the almond flour, pecan flour, sweetener, baking powder, xanthan gum, salt, and ginger and whisk until well mixed. In a large bowl, whisk the egg, sweet potato, and syrup together until thoroughly blended. Add the flour mixture and stir with a large spoon for 1 to 2 minutes to make a stiff, playdough-like dough (see page 27).

Oil your hands and gently form the mixture into small balls, using about 1/4 cup (1 1/2 oz / 42 g) of dough for each. Place the balls on the prepared pan, spacing them about 3 inches apart (to allow space for pressing down). Once all of the batter is formed into balls, rub some oil on the pinky-side edge of your hand and press down on each ball with the oiled part of your hand twice, forming a crisscross shape and slightly flattening the balls.   (CONTINUED)

Bake for 15 minutes, then rotate and bake for about 10 minutes, until golden brown and firm to the touch.

Immediately transfer the biscuits to a wire rack to cool for 3 minutes. Split and serve them while still warm.

Cooking Yams or Sweet Potatoes

Although yams and sweet potatoes are not technically the same vegetable, they are often used interchangeably by unknowing consumers. Fortunately, they are both wonderful and highly nutritious, so either will work in these biscuits.

There are a number of ways to cook yams and sweet potatoes that you intend to mash, including microwaving, boiling, or baking them in the oven. But our favorite method is steaming, which preserves the most nutrients and tenderizes them beautifully. First, peel the yam or sweet potato (one is probably more than enough for a single batch of biscuits, but it never hurts to have extra, either for more biscuits or for serving with a meal). Cut it into 8 to 10 chunks, as equal in size as possible. Fill a medium pot with enough water to come to the bottom of a steamer insert. (If you don't have a steamer insert, boil the yams or sweet potatoes directly in the water, but don't cover them—fill the pot with no more than 1 inch of water so they will steam and boil at the same time.) Place the prepared chunks in the steamer, cover the pot with a secure lid, and bring the water to a boil, lowering it to a simmer as soon as it boils. If not using a steamer, stir the pieces after 5 minutes to prevent sticking to the bottom. Steam for 10 to 20 minutes, depending on the size of your chunks, until the pieces are buttery soft and a fork pressed into the center of a piece slides through easily. Remove the pot from the heat, and carefully drain the pieces in a strainer or colander and let cool. You can use the cooked yams or sweet potatoes as soon as they cool to room temperature, or store them in the refrigerator in a covered container until you are ready to make the biscuits, removing them an hour ahead to take off the chill.

Nutty Zucchini Bread

MAKES 1 LOAF (10 TO 12 SLICES)

In this recipe, a number of interesting ingredients come together to create a unique quick bread that's moist and complexly flavored. As with most of the recipes in this book, you can substitute other nut flours to create your own variations, but in this case the coconut flour is key to the flavor and texture, so try to keep it in the mix. This bread is wonderful when toasted and served with butter, a high-quality buttery spread, or apple butter.

1/2 cup (2 oz / 57 g) walnut flour (see page 12)

1/2 cup (2 oz / 57 g) coconut flour (see Tip, page 14)

1/2 cup (2 oz / 57 g) hazelnut flour

1/2 cup (2 oz / 57 g) brown or golden flaxseed meal or hemp seed meal

1 3/4 cups Splenda or Stevia Extract in the Raw, or 3/4 cup plus 2 tablespoons New Roots Stevia Sugar

1 tablespoon baking powder

1/2 teaspoon xanthan gum

1/2 teaspoon salt

1 1/2 teaspoons ground cinnamon

1 teaspoon ground nutmeg

1 cup (3.5 oz / 99 g) walnuts, raw or lightly toasted (see Tip, page 172), chopped

2 eggs (3.5 oz / 99 g)

1/2 cup (4 oz / 113 g) unsweetened soy milk or other milk

1/4 cup (2 oz / 57 g) salted butter or margarine, melted

1 teaspoon fresh lemon juice

1 teaspoon vanilla extract

1 cup (7.25 oz / 206 g) shredded or grated zucchini, firmly packed

Preheat the oven to 350°F (177°C). Line the bottom of a 4½ by 8-inch or 5 by 9-inch loaf pan with parchment paper, then mist the pan with spray oil.

In a medium bowl, combine the walnut flour, coconut flour, hazelnut flour, flaxseed meal, sweetener, baking powder, xanthan gum, salt, cinnamon, and nutmeg. Whisk until well mixed. Stir in the walnuts. In a large bowl, whisk the eggs, milk, butter, lemon juice, and vanilla together. Stir in the zucchini. Add the flour mixture and stir with a large spoon for 1 to 2 minutes to make a thick, sticky batter (see page 27). Pour the mixture into the prepared pan.

Bake for 45 minutes, then rotate and bake for about 45 more minutes, until golden and springy when pressed in the center and a toothpick inserted into the middle of the loaf comes out clean.

Let the bread cool in the pan for about 5 minutes before carefully turning out the loaf. Let cool on a wire rack for at least 45 minutes before slicing and serving.

Mini Banana-Nut Breads

Banana bread is a perennial favorite, and this version capitalizes on the natural flavor pairing of pecans (both in flour form and chopped) and bananas. Sunflower seed flour adds yet more flavor, along with valuable nutrients. Don't be tempted to bake this bread in one big loaf; the batter is dense and doesn't get enough support in a full-size loaf pan. Besides, small loaves have the advantage that you can store them in the freezer, individually wrapped, and bring them out as needed. Because they're small, they'll thaw in less than an hour.

If you have mini loaf pans that are a different size than we call for, don't fret. Just use them and follow the doneness cues in the recipe below, adjusting the baking time as needed. Smaller loaves will bake more quickly than indicated, and larger loaves will take longer. By the way, this bread makes great toast.

1 cup (4 oz / 113 g) pecan flour (see page 12)

1 cup (4 oz / 113 g) sunflower seed flour

3/4 cup Splenda or Stevia Extract in the Raw, or 6 tablespoons New Roots Stevia Sugar

1 tablespoon baking powder

1/2 teaspoon xanthan gum

1/4 teaspoon salt

1/2 teaspoon ground cinnamon

1 cup (4 oz / 113 g) pecans, raw or lightly toasted (see Tip, page 172), chopped

4 egg whites (5 oz / 142 g)

1/4 cup (2 oz / 57 g) unsweetened soy milk or other milk

1 teaspoon vanilla extract

13/4 cups (12 oz / 340 g) mashed ripe bananas (about 2 to 3 bananas)

Preheat the oven to 375°F (191°C). Generously mist eight 2½ by 3½-inch mini loaf pans with spray oil.

In a medium bowl, combine the pecan flour, sunflower seed flour, sweetener, baking powder, xanthan gum, salt, and cinnamon and whisk until well mixed. Stir in the pecans. In a large bowl, whisk the egg whites, milk, and vanilla together until thoroughly blended. Add the flour mixture and stir with a large spoon for about 1 minute. Add the bananas and stir for 1 to 2 minutes to make a smooth, sticky batter (see page 27).

Spoon the batter into the prepared pans, distributing the batter evenly among them; they should be about three-quarters full.

Bake for 20 minutes, then rotate and bake for about 15 minutes, until golden brown and springy when pressed in the center. If baking larger loaves, note that they will take longer.

Put the pans on a wire rack and let cool for at least 5 minutes before turning out the loaves. Let cool on the wire rack for at least 10 to 20 more minutes before serving, depending on whether or not you want the bread to be warm enough to melt butter.

Chapter Five

COOKIES

It has been said by more than one baking instructor that if you want to make a living as a baker, learn how to make great cookies and you will always be able to get a job. With that in mind, here are some cookie recipes that, even if they don't land you a job, will definitely make you very popular at home.

All of these cookie recipes are straightforward and essentially foolproof. Still, we have just a few general tips to help ensure the best results:

- These cookies don't spread much during baking, so you can scoop and drop the dough onto the pan for a thick, cake-like cookie, or you can press each one down with your hand into a flatter disk for a thin, crip cookie.

- When making cookies, it's best to bake just one pan at a time. You can bake each pan sequentially or, for optimum fresh-baked flavor, chill the dough and bake more cookies at a later time. If you do bake them later, just store the batter in a tightly covered container in the refrigerator for later use, or go ahead and put the cookies on a pan, cover the pan with plastic wrap, and refrigerate until you're ready to bake. If using chilled dough, the baking time will need to be increased by a few minutes.

- With these recipes it's important to transfer the cookies to a wire rack for cooling as soon as they come out of the oven. In our experience, if they cool for even a few minutes on the pan it's much more difficult to move the cookies without breaking them.

- Although the instructions generally specify cooling the cookies for a certain amount of time, you can also enjoy them warm if you don't mind a bit of crumbling.

- Store leftover cookies in an airtight container or resealable bag, with a paper towel underneath to absorb any oil that's released. All of these cookies freeze beautifully and taste delicious straight out of the freezer, cold and crisp.

Lemon Drops

MAKES ABOUT 24 COOKIES

These delightful drop cookies are full of refreshing lemon flavor. They're delicious plain, but we recommend glazing them with the Lemon Fondant Icing for a flavor boost. You can also dust them with powdered erythritol in the style of Russian or Mexican wedding cookies, as described in the variation on page 148. One important note: Don't try to substitute vegetable oil for the butter or margarine in this recipe. It won't create the same flavor synergy with the lemon juice that you'll get with butter or a good-quality buttery spread. We highly recommend using an electric mixer for this recipe, because the dough is very thick and sticky and difficult to stir by hand.

3 cups (12 oz / 340 g) almond flour

1 1/2 cups Splenda or Stevia Extract in the Raw, or 3/4 cup New Roots Stevia Sugar

1 teaspoon baking powder

1/2 teaspoon salt

3 eggs (5.25 oz / 149 g)

1/4 cup (2 oz / 57 g) salted butter or margarine, melted

1/4 cup (2 oz / 57 g) fresh lemon juice

1 1/2 teaspoons lemon extract

1/2 teaspoon liquid stevia

Lemon Fondant Icing

2/3 cup powered erythritol, Stevia Extract in the Raw, or Splenda, or 1/3 cup New Roots Stevia Sugar

2 tablespoons fresh lemon juice

Position 2 oven racks in the middle of the oven. Preheat the oven to 350°F (177°C). Mist 2 baking sheets with spray oil, or line them with parchment paper or silicone mats and then lightly mist the surfaces with spray oil.

In a medium bowl, combine the almond flour, Splenda, baking powder, and salt and whisk until well mixed. In a large bowl, whisk the eggs, butter, lemon juice, lemon extract, and liquid stevia together until thoroughly blended. Add the flour mixture and stir with a large spoon for 1 to 2 minutes to make a very thick, sticky batter (see page 27). Scrape down the sides of the bowl and stir for 30 seconds.

Drop the dough onto the prepared pans, using about 1 heaping tablespoon of dough per cookie; alternatively, lightly grease your hands and roll the portions of dough into balls. Space the cookies about 3 inches apart (measured from the center of each cookie).

Bake for 8 minutes, then rotate the pans and switch racks and bake for 6 to 8 minutes, until the cookies are light golden brown and firm to the touch.   (CONTINUED)

Meanwhile, make the lemon fondant icing (which is optional). In a small bowl, combine the erythritol and lemon juice and whisk until thoroughly blended.

Let the cookies cool on the pan for about 3 minutes. While they're still on the pan, brush the tops with the icing; alternatively, you can dip the cookies into the fondant to coat the tops.

Put the glazed cookies on a wire rack and let cool for at least 15 minutes before serving (this also allows the fondant to set up).

VARIATION

Lemon Wedding Cookies: Omit the glaze and dust the cookies with erythritol instead. (Be sure to use powdered, not granular erythritol; see Resources for more information.) Put ½ cup of powdered erythritol in a small, shallow dish. While the cookies are still warm, gently swirl the top of each in the erythritol powder, then return them to the wire rack to cool completely.

Butter-Almond Cookies

MAKES ABOUT 24 COOKIES

This is a very versatile all-purpose cookie that can be jazzed up in a variety of ways, making a great foundation for experimentation. For example, you could substitute different sweet spices, such as ginger, allspice, or nutmeg, for the cinnamon (as long as the total doesn't exceed 1 teaspoon). You can also replace the sliced almonds with other chopped nuts, or add some toasted coconut, as in the variation below.

2 cups (8 oz / 227 g) almond flour

1 cup Splenda or Stevia Extract in the Raw, or 1/2 cup New Roots Stevia Sugar

1/2 teaspoon baking soda

1/4 teaspoon salt

1 teaspoon ground cinnamon (optional)

2/3 cup (2.25 oz / 64 g) sliced almonds

1 egg (1.75 oz / 50 g)

3/4 cup (6 oz / 170 g) salted butter or margarine, melted

1 tablespoon vanilla extract

Position 2 oven racks in the middle of the oven. Preheat the oven to 350°F (177°C). Lightly mist 2 baking sheets with spray oil, or line them with parchment paper or silicone mats and then lightly mist the surfaces with spray oil.

In a medium bowl, combine the almond flour, sweetener, baking soda, salt, and cinnamon and whisk until well mixed. Stir in the almonds. In a large bowl, whisk the egg, butter, and vanilla together until thoroughly blended. Add the flour mixture and stir with a large spoon for 1 to 2 minutes to make a thick, sticky dough (see page 27).

Drop the dough onto the prepared pans, using about 1 heaping tablespoon of dough per cookie and spacing them about 3 inches apart.

Bake for 9 minutes, then rotate the pans and switch racks and bake for about 9 more minutes, until the cookies are firm to the touch and golden brown. (If you prefer crunchy cookies, leave them in the oven for about 2 more minutes.)

Transfer the cookies to a wire rack and let cool for at least 10 minutes before serving.

VARIATION

Coconut Butter Cookies: Add 1/2 cup (1.25 oz / 35 g) unsweetened coconut flakes, lightly toasted (see Tip, page 150), when you add the almonds.

Coconut-Pecan Cookies

MAKES ABOUT 24 COOKIES

These chewy, macaroon-like cookies have a wonderful flavor harmony from the pecan flour, coconut flakes, and coconut flour. Finely ground coconut flour with the consistency of powdered sugar is best for this recipe. Grind yours as fine as possible.

1 cup (4 oz / 113 g) pecan flour (see page 12)

1¼ cups (5 oz / 142 g) coconut flour (see Tip, page 14)

1½ cups Splenda or Stevia Extract in the Raw, or ¾ cup New Roots Stevia Sugar

2 teaspoons baking powder

½ cup (1.25 oz / 35 g) unsweetened coconut flakes, lightly toasted (see Tip)

1 egg (1.75 oz / 50 g)

½ cup (4 oz / 113 g) soy milk or other milk

¼ cup (2 oz / 57 g) sugar-free maple-flavored syrup

1 tablespoon vanilla extract

Position 2 oven racks in the middle of the oven. Preheat the oven to 350°F (177°C). Line 2 baking sheets with parchment paper or silicone mats, then lightly mist the surfaces with spray oil.

In a medium bowl, combine the pecan flour, coconut flour, sweetener, and baking powder and whisk until well mixed. Stir in the coconut flakes. In a large bowl, whisk the egg, milk, syrup, and vanilla together until thoroughly blended. Add the flour mixture and stir with a large spoon for 1 to 2 minutes to make a thick, sticky batter (see page 27).

Drop the dough onto the prepared pans, using about 1 heaping tablespoon of dough per cookie and spacing them about 3 inches apart.

Bake for 6 minutes, then rotate the pans and switch racks, and bake for 6 to 8 minutes, until golden brown and firm to the touch.

Let the cookies cool on the pan for 5 to 7 minutes, then transfer to a wire rack.

Tip: Toasting Coconut

To toast coconut flakes or shredded coconut, put it in a dry skillet over medium heat and cook, stirring frequently, until the coconut begins to brown slightly and release a pleasant coconut aroma. Immediately remove it from the hot pan to prevent burning.

You can also toast it under the broiler. Spread it on a rimmed baking sheet and place it on the lower rack of the oven. Stir the coconut or shake the pan from time to time, and monitor it closely so it doesn't burn.

Hazelnut-Vanilla Cookies

MAKES ABOUT 24 COOKIES

These basic vanilla cookies have a pleasant flavor reminiscent of gianduja—the ever-popular blend of chocolate and hazelnuts. They are wonderful for any occasion and a nice accompaniment to a cup of hot tea or a mug of hot chocolate (sugar-free, of course).

2 cups (8 oz / 227 g) hazelnut flour

1 cup (4 oz / 113 g) almond flour

1 1/2 cups Splenda or Stevia Extract in the Raw, or 3/4 cup plus 2 tablespoons New Roots Stevia Sugar

2 teaspoons baking powder

1/2 teaspoon cream of tartar

1/4 teaspoon xanthan gum

2 eggs (3.5 oz / 99 g)

1/2 cup (4 oz / 113 g) soy milk or other milk

1/4 cup (2 oz / 57 g) salted butter or margarine, melted

2 tablespoons vanilla extract

1/4 teaspoon liquid stevia

Position 2 oven racks in the middle of the oven. Preheat the oven to 375°F (191°C). Mist 2 baking sheets with spray oil, or line them with parchment paper or silicone mats and then mist the surfaces with spray oil.

In a medium bowl, combine the hazelnut flour, almond flour, Splenda, baking powder, cream of tartar, and xanthan gum and whisk until well mixed. In a large bowl, whisk the eggs, milk, butter, vanilla, and liquid stevia together until thoroughly blended. Add the flour mixture and stir with a large spoon for 1 to 2 minutes to make a thick, sticky batter (see page 27).

Drop the dough onto the prepared pans, using about 1 heaping tablespoon of dough per cookie and spacing them about 3 inches apart.

Bake for 9 minutes, then rotate the pans and switch racks and bake for about 9 more minutes, until the cookies are golden brown and firm to the touch.

Immediately transfer the cookies to a wire rack and let cool for at least 15 minutes before serving.

VARIATIONS

Nutty Vanilla Cookies: For crunchier cookies, add 1/2 cup of chopped pecans (1.75 oz / 50 g) or almonds or hazelnuts (about 2.5 oz / 71 g) when mixing the dry ingredients.

Chocolaty Vanilla Cookies: For that gianduja flavor, add up to 1 cup of sugar-free chocolate chips (see page 21) to the dry ingredients.

Thumbprint Jam Cookies

MAKES ABOUT 24 COOKIES

These easy cookies are a lot of fun to make with kids. Helpers can make their own thumbprints and then fill them with their favorite sugar-free jam.

2¹/₂ cups (10 oz / 283 g) almond flour

1 cup (4 oz / 113 g) coconut flour (see Tip, page 14)

1¹/₂ cups Splenda or Stevia Extract in the Raw, or ³/₄ cup New Roots Stevia Sugar

1¹/₂ teaspoons baking powder

¹/₂ teaspoon salt

3 eggs (5.25 oz / 149 g)

¹/₂ cup (4 oz / 113 g) salted butter or margarine, melted

4 teaspoons vanilla extract

About 6 tablespoons (3.5 oz / 99 g) sugar-free jelly or jam

Position 2 oven racks in the middle of the oven. Preheat the oven to 350°F (177°C). Lightly mist 2 baking sheets with spray oil, or line them with parchment paper or silicone mats and then lightly mist the surfaces with spray oil.

In a medium bowl, combine the almond flour, coconut flour, sweetener, baking powder, and salt and whisk until well mixed. In a large bowl, whisk the eggs, butter, and vanilla together. Add the flour mixture and stir with a large spoon for 1 to 2 minutes to make a stiff, playdough-like dough (see page 27).

To form each cookie, scoop out 1 heaping tablespoon of dough and, using oiled hands, roll it into a ball, then press it gently between your palms to flatten it slightly. Place the cookies on the prepared pans, spacing them 3 inches apart. Press your thumb into the center of each cookie to make an indentation. Spoon ½ teaspoon of the jelly into each indentation.

Bake for 8 minutes, then rotate the pans and switch racks and bake for 8 to 10 minutes, until golden and firm to the touch.

Immediately transfer the cookies to a wire rack and let cool for at least 15 minutes before serving to allow the jam to cool.

Seriously Chocolate Pecan Cookies

MAKES ABOUT 24 COOKIES

These cookies have enough cocoa to satisfy even the most serious chocolate craving. Dutch-process cocoa powder yields darker cookies than standard cocoa powder, but either way, these cookies will be excellent. Serving them with a glass of cold milk is highly recommended! Or, for a highly indulgent treat, serve them warm, right out of the oven, with sugar-free ice cream, garnished with a bit of Sugar-Free Whipped Cream (see page 202) or nondairy topping—or whatever embellishments you desire—to create an instant chocolate cookie sundae. A final possibility is dusting the cookies with powdered erythritol for a sweet, snowy topping. For instructions on doing so, see the variation on page 148.

2 cups (8 oz / 227 g) pecan flour (see page 12)

1 cup (4 oz / 113 g) almond flour

2 cups Splenda or Stevia Extract in the Raw, or 1 cup New Roots Stevia Sugar

3/4 cup (2.25 oz / 64 g) unsweetened cocoa powder, natural or Dutch-process

2 teaspoons baking powder

1/4 teaspoon salt

1/2 cup (1.75 oz / 50 g) pecans, coarsely chopped

3 eggs (5.25 oz / 149 g)

1/4 cup (2 oz / 57 g) salted butter or margarine, melted

4 teaspoons vanilla extract

1/4 teaspoon liquid stevia

Position 2 oven racks in the middle of the oven. Preheat the oven to 350°F (177°C). Mist 2 baking sheets with spray oil, or line them with parchment paper or silicone mats and then mist the surfaces with spray oil.

In a medium bowl, combine the pecan flour, almond flour, Splenda, cocoa powder, baking powder, and salt and whisk until well mixed. Stir in the pecans. In a large bowl, whisk the eggs, butter, vanilla, and liquid stevia together until thoroughly blended. Add the flour mixture and stir with a large spoon for about 2 minutes to make a thick, sticky batter (see page 27).

Drop the dough onto the prepared pans, using about 1 heaping tablespoon of dough per cookie and spacing them about 3 inches apart.

Bake for 8 minutes, then rotate the pans and switch racks and bake for 6 to 8 minutes, until the cookies are firm to the touch and crispy.

Immediately transfer the cookies to a wire rack and let cool for at least 15 minutes before serving.

Nutty Peanut Butter Cookies

MAKES ABOUT 24 COOKIES

Yes, three ways of using peanuts in one recipe! These delicious cookies are perfect as an after-school treat or dessert for peanut butter fans. You can use either crunchy or smooth peanut butter, but note that the amount of milk in the batter varies depending on which type you use. Serve these cookies warm or cold, with a tall glass of cold milk. For a super-indulgent treat, use this recipe to make the Inside-Out Peanut Butter Cup Cookies on page 158.

1¹/₂ cups (6 oz / 170 g) almond flour

²/₃ cup (3.25 oz / 92 g) peanut flour

¹/₂ cup (2 oz / 57 g) coconut flour (see Tip, page 14)

1 cup Splenda or Stevia Extract in the Raw, or ¹/₂ cup New Roots Stevia Sugar

1 teaspoon baking powder

¹/₄ teaspoon salt

¹/₂ cup (2 oz / 57 g) chopped roasted peanuts

1 egg (1.75 oz / 50 g)

1 cup (9.75 oz / 276 g) sugar-free peanut butter, crunchy or smooth

1 cup (8 oz / 227 g) soy milk or other milk

¹/₄ cup (2 oz / 60 ml) sugar-free maple-flavored syrup

2¹/₂ teaspoons vanilla extract

1¹/₄ teaspoons liquid stevia

Position 2 oven racks in the middle of the oven. Preheat the oven to 375°F (191°C). Line 2 baking sheets with parchment paper or silicone mats, then mist the surface with spray oil.

In a medium bowl, combine the almond flour, peanut flour, coconut flour, Splenda, baking powder, and salt and whisk until well mixed. Stir in the chopped peanuts. In a large bowl or the bowl of an electric mixer, combine the egg, peanut butter, milk, syrup, vanilla, and liquid stevia and stir vigorously with a large spoon or mix with the paddle attachment at medium-low speed until thoroughly blended. Add the flour mixture and stir vigorously or mix at medium speed until all of the ingredients are evenly combined. The batter will be a thick, sticky dough (see page 27).

Drop the dough onto the prepared pans, using about 1 heaping tablespoon of dough per cookie; alternatively, lightly grease your hands and roll the portions of dough into balls. Space the cookies about 3 inches apart. Use the back of the tines of a fork and lightly press to form a cross-hatch design and slightly flatten the cookies. Dip the fork in cold water as needed to prevent sticking.

Bake for 6 minutes, then rotate the pans and switch racks and bake for about 6 more minutes, until the cookies are firm to the touch. For crunchier cookies, bake for about 2 more minutes.

Immediately transfer the cookies to a wire rack and let cool for at least 10 minutes before serving.

VARIATION

Peanut Butter Cookie and Ice Cream Sandwiches: For a fun snack for kids and adults alike, put a small scoop of slightly softened sugar-free vanilla ice cream between 2 of the cookies. Press gently to distribute the ice cream. Then, return to the freezer for at least 10 minutes before serving. Why not make a few and keep them in the freezer for times when you need a special treat?

Inside-Out Peanut Butter Cup Cookies

MAKES 12 LARGE COOKIES

For those of us who shouldn't eat candy for health reasons (and isn't that most of us?), these cookies help fulfill the craving for chocolate-covered peanut butter cups. To take them over the top, drizzle Chocolate Glaze (page 162) over the baked and cooled cookies. We call for baking the cookies in muffin cups, but you could also use a 12-compartment mini loaf pan. For sugar-free chocolate syrup, Denene uses the Publix store brand because it has the fewest carbs. Hershey's and Smucker's also make sugar-free chocolate syrup, but the carbs are slightly higher. Look over the options at your market and get the one with the lowest total amount of carbs.

1 batch unbaked Nutty Peanut Butter Cookie dough (page 156)

Chocolate Filling

1 cup (8.75 oz / 248 g) sugar-free chocolate syrup

1 teaspoon vanilla extract

1/4 teaspoon liquid stevia

1 envelope (0.25 oz / 7 g) unflavored powdered gelatin, or 1 teaspoon agar flakes

Preheat the oven to 400°F (204°C). Mist 12 muffin cups with spray oil. Have the cookie dough ready.

To make the filling, whisk the syrup, vanilla, liquid stevia, and gelatin together in a medium bowl until thoroughly blended. Let the mixture sit for 3 to 5 minutes to allow the gelatin to expand and bloom. Whisk the mixture periodically as you fill the cookies to keep the gelatin evenly distributed.

Put 1 heaping tablespoon of the cookie dough into each prepared muffin cup. Oil your fingers and press the dough into the walls of the cup to form a ¼-inch-thick crust, just like a mini pie shell. Use only as much dough as needed to make a thin crust; the remaining dough will be used in a subsequent step.

Spoon the chocolate mixture into the muffin cups, dividing it evenly among them.

Mist a work surface with spray oil and transfer the remaining cookie dough to the oiled spot. Divide the dough into 12 equal portions. Oil your hands and roll each portion into a ball. Set the balls on the oiled work surface and press them with the palm of your hand until large enough to cover the cookie crusts. Set the disks atop the chocolate and crimp the edges of the top and bottom cookie crusts together to completely encase the chocolate centers. (CONTINUED)

Bake for 15 minutes, then rotate and bake for about 15 more minutes, until the top crust is golden and firm to the touch. Don't worry if some of the chocolate centers ooze out during the baking process. The chocolate can easily be scraped off the pan (and eaten, of course!) once the cookies are baked.

Put the pan on a wire rack and let the cookies cool for at least 20 minutes, until completely cool before turning them out.

Pecan Sandies

MAKES ABOUT 24 COOKIES

Sandies are a classic butter cookie with pecans—a delicious combination. This is one of Denene's favorite recipes; she recommends making lots of these cookies and sharing them with everyone!

1 cup (4 oz / 113 g) pecan flour (see page 12)

1 cup (4 oz / 113 g) almond flour

1 cup Splenda or Stevia Extract in the Raw, or ¹/₂ cup New Roots Stevia Sugar

¹/₂ teaspoon baking soda

¹/₄ teaspoon salt

1 cup (3.5 oz / 99 g) pecans, chopped

1 egg (1.75 oz / 50 g)

³/₄ cup (6 oz / 170 g) salted butter or margarine, melted

1 tablespoon vanilla extract

Position 2 oven racks in the middle of the oven. Preheat the oven to 350°F (177°C). Line 2 baking sheets with parchment paper or silicone mats, then lightly mist the surfaces with spray oil.

In a medium bowl, combine the pecan flour, almond flour, sweetener, baking soda, and salt and whisk until well mixed. Stir in the pecans. In a large bowl, whisk the egg, butter, and vanilla together until thoroughly blended. Add the flour mixture and stir with a large spoon for 1 to 2 minutes to make a thick, sticky batter (see page 27).

Drop the dough onto the prepared pans, using about 1 heaping tablespoon per cookie and spacing them 3 inches apart.

Bake for 9 minutes, then rotate the pans and switch racks and bake about 9 more minutes, until the cookies are golden brown and firm to the touch.

Immediately transfer the cookies to a wire rack and let cool for at least 10 minutes before serving.

Biscotti

These gluten-free, sugar-free biscotti rival classic versions made with wheat flour; in fact, in our estimation, their snap and crumble factors and flavors are superior. Biscotti, by definition, are twice-baked cookies, first baked as a soft, mounded loaf, and then sliced and baked again until crisp. They are often used as dipping cookies in coffee, tea, hot chocolate, or even wine. This recipe yields good dippers, but they can stand on their own as one of the most addictive, guilt-free treats you will ever enjoy. Store some of them hidden away in the freezer, as you will be tempted to consume them all if they aren't out of sight and out of mind.

1 cup (4 oz / 113 g) pecan flour (see page 12)

1 cup (4 oz / 113 g) almond flour

1/4 cup (1 oz / 28 g) coconut flour (see Tip, page 14)

1 cup Splenda or Stevia Extract in the Raw, or 1/2 cup New Roots Stevia Sugar

2 teaspoons baking powder

4 egg whites (5 oz / 142 g)

1 tablespoon vanilla extract

1/3 cup (2.75 oz / 78 g) salted butter or margarine, melted

1 1/2 cups (7.5 oz / 213 g) almonds, coarsely chopped

Chocolate Glaze

1 cup (6 oz / 170 g) sugar-free semisweet chocolate chips or chopped chocolate

2 tablespoons (1 oz / 28 g) salted butter (or butter substitute), or soy milk if using ChocoPerfection brand chocolate

Preheat the oven to 400°F (204°C). Line a baking sheet with parchment paper or a silicone mat, then lightly mist the surface with spray oil.

In a medium bowl, combine the pecan flour, almond flour, coconut flour, sweetener, and baking powder and whisk until well mixed. In a large bowl, whisk the egg whites and vanilla together until thoroughly blended, then add the butter and whisk for a few seconds, until thoroughly blended. Add the flour mixture and stir with a large spoon for 1 to 2 minutes to make a thick, sticky dough that is moldable (see page 27). Stir in the chopped almonds until evenly distributed.

Use a rubber spatula to transfer the dough to the center of the prepared pan. Using the spatula or wet hands, form it into either 1 large oval about 6 inches wide and 10 to 12 inches long, or 2 smaller ovals about 4 inches wide and 8 inches long. Regardless of size, the ovals should be about ¾ inch tall.   (CONTINUED)

Bake for 15 minutes, then rotate and bake for 10 to 15 minutes, until golden brown and and still springy when pressed in the center. (It's important not to overbake at this point, or the loaves will be too difficult to slice.)

Let cool on the pan for 2 minutes, then, while the loaf or loaves are still hot, use a chef's knife to cut them into ¾-inch slices on a diagonal across the oval. (If the loaves cool too much, they will harden and the pieces will shatter and fall apart when sliced.) Use a metal or plastic spatula to transfer the slices to a wire rack, flat side down, spacing them about ½ inch apart. If you can't fit them all on one wire rack, use two.

Lower the oven temperature to 275°F (135°C). Put the wire rack with the biscotti back into the oven—rack, biscotti, and all—and bake for 15 minutes. Remove the wire rack, flip the biscotti over (only if necessary for even coloring), then bake for 15 to 20 minutes, or as needed, until all sides of the biscotti are golden brown and feel crisp.

Let the biscotti cool on the rack for about 45 minutes, or until completely cool.

Meanwhile, make the chocolate glaze. Combine the chocolate and butter in the top of a double boiler and cook over simmering water, stirring occasionally, until melted and smooth. Alternatively, you can combine them in a microwave-safe bowl and microwave at medium heat. The chocolate will melt quickly in the microwave and will be damaged if it overheats, so use short, 15-second intervals and stir in between. Once the chocolate is almost melted, use even shorter intervals.

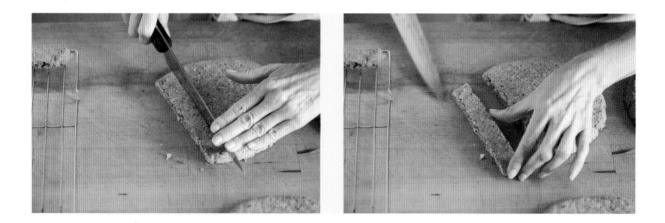

Alternate Methods for Applying Chocolate Glaze

To drizzle the glaze over the biscotti in a decorative pattern, use a rubber spatula to transfer the glaze into a plastic sandwich bag or disposable piping bag. Work the chocolate into one corner of the bag and, if using a plastic bag, cut a tiny tip off of that corner. Pipe the chocolate onto one flat side of all of the biscotti in a crisscross pattern. You can also drizzle the melted chocolate off the end of a spoon or spatula in squiggles. Let sit until the chocolate hardens.

You can also use a pastry brush, rubber spatula, or icing spatula to spread chocolate across one flat side of the biscotti for a more solid glaze. Again, let the biscotti sit until the chocolate hardens.

When the biscotti are completely cool to the touch, dip one or both ends of each into the chocolate glaze. Return them to the wire rack and let sit until the chocolate hardens (or, if you can't wait that long, set a few in the refrigerator to hasten the process). See the sidebar above for alternative methods of applying the chocolate glaze.

VARIATION

Chocolate Biscotti: If you can eat standard chocolate, sweetened with sugar, melt ¼ cup (2 oz / 57 g) of butter or butter substitute with the chocolate chips, instead of 2 tablespoons, to make the glaze more fluid.

Chapter Six

BROWNIES, CAKES, AND COFFEE CAKES

Cakes are often the highlight of a cookbook (at least in the estimation of the end users—the eaters). Our guess is that it will probably hold true for this book as well. They are also essential for birthdays and other celebrations, and sharing them is part of the occasion. Unfortunately, those who are diabetic or sensitive to gluten are often left on the sidelines. But no more! The recipes in this chapter yield decadent, satisfying cakes that almost everyone can enjoy.

Once you've mastered any of the cakes in this chapter, you can use the recipe as a foundation for creating your own unique variations on a delicious theme by using different types of nut and seed flours in different proportions. Here are some tips and ideas about variations that apply to all of the recipes in this chapter:

- Because various brands of nut flours, levels of grind, and types of nuts absorb liquid differently, you may need to adjust these recipes by adding more liquid or nut flour to achieve the batter texture we describe.

- Most of the cakes can be baked in different pans than those called for. Springform tube pans, Bundt pans, and standard tube pans are all essentially interchangeable, with springform tube pans being easier to remove and therefore the best bet for stickier cakes. Springform tube pans are also great for cakes with crumb toppings; when these are made in a Bundt pan, they're typically inverted for serving, so the crumb topping ends up on the bottom. With a springform tube pan, you can keep the topping on top.

- Cakes that call for tube-style pans can also be made in standard round cake pans or square or rectangular pans, but baking times will vary depending on the size and shape of the pan chosen. When substituting pans, make sure the alternative pan or pans have a total volume similar to the size of pan we call for, and then follow the doneness cues, rather than baking times, to assess when baking is complete.

- All of the cakes in this chapter are delicious whether served warm, at room temperature, or cold.

- Because these cakes are made with nut and seed flours, which contain substantial amounts of oil, they are more perishable than many conventional baked goods. Be sure to store any leftovers, tightly covered or wrapped, in the refrigerator or freezer. In the refrigerator, they'll typically keep for about 7 to 10 days; in the freezer, they'll keep for several months.

- These cakes have a tendency to stick to the pan more than standard cakes, so we've provided special pan preparation in this chapter. Greasing the pan, freezing it, then dusting with coconut flour or almond flour is a sure-fire way to have every cake come out of the pan cleanly and intact. (Coconut flour has the consistency of powdered sugar and it sticks best to the frozen butter; almond flour is fine if you don't have coconut flour.) If baking in a standard round cake pan or loaf pan, you can also cut out baking parchment to fit the bottom of the pan, then mist it with spray oil.

Cocoa-Nut Brownies

MAKES 12 BROWNIES

There is nothing quite like the satisfaction of biting into a warm chocolate brownie, and this recipe makes a wonderful, guilt-free version. For added indulgence, serve these brownies with sugar-free ice cream. Or win some popularity points by packing them into bagged lunches—including your own! Note that this recipe is written to use unsweetened chocolate soy milk or almond milk. If you happen to find a sugar-free sweetened chocolate milk, or if sugar isn't an issue and you use sweetened chocolate milk, omit the liquid stevia.

2 cups (8 oz / 227 g) pecan flour (see page 12)

1 cup (4 oz / 113 g) almond flour

2 cups Splenda or Stevia Extract in the Raw, or 1/2 cup New Roots Stevia Sugar

1/2 cup (1.5 oz / 43 g) unsweetened natural cocoa powder (not Dutch-process)

2 teaspoons baking powder

3 eggs (5.25 oz / 149 g)

1/2 cup (4 oz / 113 g) unsweetened chocolate soy milk or chocolate almond milk

1/4 cup (2 oz / 57 g) salted butter or margarine, melted

1 tablespoon vanilla extract

1/2 teaspoon liquid stevia

Preheat the oven to 350°F (177°C). Line the bottom of an 8-inch square baking pan with parchment paper, then mist the pan with spray oil.

In a medium bowl, combine the pecan flour, almond flour, Splenda, cocoa powder, and baking powder and whisk until well mixed. In a large bowl, whisk the eggs, soy milk, butter, vanilla, and liquid stevia together until thoroughly blended. Add the flour mixture and whisk or stir with a large spoon until all of the ingredients are evenly incorporated to make a smooth, sticky batter (see page 27).

Pour the mixture into the prepared pan, spreading it in an even layer if need be. Bake for 15 minutes, then rotate and bake for 10 minutes, until the brownies are just slightly springy but still jiggly when pressed gently in the center. If you like fudgy brownies, remove them from the oven at this point. If you prefer them to be more cakelike, continue baking for a few more minutes, until a toothpick inserted into the middle of the brownies comes out clean.   (CONTINUED)

COCOA-NUT BROWNIES, *continued*

Let the brownies cool in the pan for at least 15 minutes. You can either cut the brownies in the pan, or transfer the whole piece to a cutting board before cutting. Cut them in a 3 by 4 grid, to yield 12 brownies.

VARIATIONS

Nutty Brownies: For another layer of texture and flavor, add ½ cup (1.75 oz / 50 g) pecans or walnuts, lightly toasted (see Tip, page 172) and chopped, when mixing the dry ingredients.

Chocolate-Glazed Brownies: Once the brownies are completely cool, spread Chocolate Glaze (page 162) evenly over the top.

Pumpkin and Pumpkin Seed Blondies

MAKES 9 LARGE OR 16 SMALL BLONDIES

These spiced bar cookies have the consistency of a chewy brownie, but without the cocoa. To up the flavor factor, serve them with a dollop of Sugar-Free Whipped Cream (page 202) and a dusting of ground cinnamon.

1 1/2 cups (6 oz / 170 g) hazelnut flour

1/2 cup (2 oz / 57 g) pecan flour (see page 12)

1 1/2 cups Splenda or Stevia Extract in the Raw, or 3/4 cup New Roots Stevia Sugar

2 teaspoons baking powder

1 teaspoon xanthan gum

1/2 teaspoon salt

1 teaspoon ground cinnamon

1/2 teaspoon ground ginger

1/4 teaspoon ground cloves (optional)

2 eggs (3.5 oz / 99 g)

1 can (15 oz / 425 g) unsweetened pumpkin puree

2 teaspoons vanilla extract

1/2 cup (3 oz / 85 g) coarsely chopped pumpkin seeds or sunflower seeds, lightly toasted (see Tip, page 172)

Preheat the oven to 360°F (182°C). Line the bottom of an 8-inch square baking pan with parchment paper, then mist the pan with spray oil.

In a medium bowl, combine the hazelnut flour, pecan flour, sweetener, baking powder, xanthan gum, salt, cinnamon, ginger, and cloves and whisk until well mixed. In a large bowl, whisk the eggs, pumpkin, and vanilla together until thoroughly blended. Add the flour mixture and stir with a large spoon for 1 to 2 minutes to make a smooth, sticky batter (see page 27). Fold in the pumpkin seeds.

Use a spoon or rubber spatula to transfer the batter to the prepared pan, then spread it in an even layer. Bake for 30 minutes, then rotate the dish and bake for about 30 more minutes, until springy when pressed in the center and a toothpick inserted into the middle of the blondies comes out clean.

Let the blondies cool in the pan for at least 15 minutes. (You can either cut the blondies in the pan or transfer the whole piece to a cutting board first.) Cut into 9 large squares or 16 small squares and serve.   (CONTINUED)

PUMPKIN AND PUMPKIN SEED BLONDIES, *continued*

VARIATIONS

Blondies with Cream Cheese Frosting: Once the blondies are completely cool, spread Cream Cheese Frosting (page 184) evenly over the top.

Blondie Ice Cream Sandwiches: For a treat kids of all ages will enjoy, slice a blondie horizontally, then put a small scoop of slightly softened sugar-free ice cream between the 2 halves. Press gently to distribute the ice cream. Place back into the freezer for 10 minutes, then serve. While you're at it, make a few and store them in the freezer for those times when you need a special treat.

Tip: Toasting Seeds and Nuts

Here's an easy way to toast pumpkin seeds, sunflower seeds, and sesame seeds: Preheat the broiler. Spread the seeds on a rimmed baking sheet in an even layer and toast them on the lowest rack of the oven for just 2 to 3 minutes. (Nuts may take a bit longer.) Watch them closely, as they can easily burn. When they get just a bit darker and smell aromatic, they're done. You can also toast seeds in a dry skillet over medium-high heat, stirring frequently, until they start to pop. Keep stirring them or shaking the pan for a minute or two, until the pan cools down, or transfer the seeds to a bowl or other container to stop the cooking process.

Hazelnut-Coconut Coffee Cake

MAKES 10 TO 12 SERVINGS

In this cake, a double dose of coconut flavor from both coconut flakes and coconut milk nicely complements the flavor of the hazelnut flour. All cakes are good with a cup of coffee, but that's particularly true of this one. It's also wonderful with a dollop of Sugar-Free Whipped Cream (page 202) or a scoop of sugar-free coffee ice cream.

3 cups (12 oz / 340 g) hazelnut flour, plus more for dusting the pan

1½ cups Splenda or Stevia Extract in the Raw, or ¾ cup New Roots Stevia Sugar

1 tablespoon baking powder

½ teaspoon xanthan gum

½ teaspoon salt

¾ cup (1.85 oz / 52 g) unsweetened coconut flakes, toasted (see Tip, page 150)

4 eggs (7 oz / 198 g)

1 cup (8 oz / 227 g) unsweetened coconut milk or any type of milk

¼ cup (2 oz / 57 g) salted butter or margarine, melted

½ teaspoon liquid stevia

Preheat the oven to 375°F (191°C). Grease a Bundt pan entirely with butter or margarine (see page 167) and place it in the freezer.

In a medium bowl, combine the hazelnut flour, Splenda, baking powder, xanthan gum, and salt and whisk until well mixed. Stir in the coconut flakes. In a large bowl, whisk the eggs, coconut milk, butter, and liquid stevia together until thoroughly combined. Add the flour mixture and stir with a large spoon for 1 to 2 minutes to make a thick, sticky batter (see page 27).

Remove your prepared pan from the freezer, then dust the entire inner surface with hazelnut flour. Pour the mixture into the prepared pan and jiggle it to evenly distribute the batter into every nook and cranny. Bake for 30 minutes, then rotate and bake for about 25 minutes, until springy when pressed in the center and a toothpick inserted into the middle of the cake comes out clean.

Let the cake cool in the pan for 20 minutes before turning it out onto a wire rack. Let cool for at least 20 more minutes before slicing and serving.

VARIATION

Nutty Coconut Coffee Cake: To add more texture to the cake, stir in ½ cup (about 2.5 oz / 71 g) of almonds or hazelnuts, lightly toasted (see Tip, page 172) and chopped, when you stir in the coconut flakes.

Very Vanilla Coffee Cake with Nut Streusel

MAKES 12 SERVINGS

Vanilla must be the most beloved flavor and aroma in the world, and this coffee cake delivers it in full force. A springform tube pan is best here, but if you don't have one, you can use a Bundt pan or a regular tube pan.

3 cups (12 oz / 340 g) almond flour, plus more for dusting the pan

1 cup (4 oz / 113 g) pecan flour, walnut flour, or hazelnut flour (see page 12)

2 cups Splenda or Stevia Extract in the Raw, or 1 cup New Roots Stevia Sugar

1½ teaspoons baking powder

¼ teaspoon salt

5 eggs (8.75 oz / 248 g)

1 cup (8 oz / 227 g) unsweetened soy milk or other milk

¼ cup (2 oz / 57 g) salted butter or margarine, melted

2 tablespoons vanilla extract

¼ teaspoon liquid stevia

Streusel Topping

1 cup pecans, walnuts, hazelnuts, or almonds, lightly toasted (see Tip, page 172) and coarsely chopped

¼ cup Splenda, Stevia Extract in the Raw, Truvia, or ZSweet, or 2 tablespoons New Roots Stevia Sugar

¼ teaspoon ground cinnamon (optional)

Preheat the oven to 350°F (177°C). Grease a springform tube pan entirely with butter or margarine (see page 167) and place it in the freezer.

In a medium bowl, combine the almond flour, pecan flour, Splenda, baking powder, and salt and whisk until well mixed. In a large bowl, whisk the eggs, milk, butter, vanilla, and liquid stevia together until thoroughly blended. Add the flour mixture and stir with a large spoon for 1 to 2 minutes to make a thick, sticky batter (see page 27).

Remove your prepared pan from the freezer, then dust the entire inner surface with almond flour. Pour the mixture into the prepared pan and smooth the top with a rubber spatula.

To make the topping, combine all of the ingredients in a small bowl and stir until thoroughly combined. Sprinkle the topping evenly over the batter, then lightly press the chopped nuts to embed them.

Bake for 30 minutes, then rotate and bake for 30 to 40 minutes, until the cake is golden brown and springy when pressed in the center and a toothpick inserted into the middle of the cake comes out clean.

Let the cake cool for 10 to 15 minutes, then remove the outer ring. Let cool for at least 15 more minutes before slicing and serving. *Note:* If using a Bundt pan or tube pan rather than a springform pan, invert the pan onto a platter or wire rack after the first 5 minutes of cooling. Let it cool for 15 more minutes before carefully removing the pan, then let it cool for at least 15 more minutes before slicing and serving.

VARIATION

Caffe Latte Coffee Cake: Add up to 1 tablespoon of instant coffee crystals when mixing the dry ingredients.

Vanilla Coffee Cake with Yogurt Topping: Spread plain yogurt over the cake after it cools; the tanginess of the yogurt provides a wonderful flavor contrast to the sweetness of the cake. If you plan to use this topping, the streusel is optional.

Cinnamon-Raisin Coffee Cake

MAKES 12 SERVINGS

This delicious coffee cake is extremely easy to make. If you're sensitive to the sugar in dried fruit, stick with just 1/4 cup (1.25 oz / 35 g) of raisins; if not, you can increase the amount to as much as 1 cup (5 oz / 142 g). Also, feel free to substitute dried cranberries or other dried fruit for the raisins.

2 cups (8 oz / 227 g) hazelnut flour

2 cups (8 oz / 227 g) almond flour, plus more for dusting the pan

1/2 cup Splenda or Stevia Extract in the Raw, or 1/4 cup New Roots Stevia Sugar

1 1/2 teaspoons baking powder

1/4 teaspoon salt

1/2 teaspoon ground cinnamon

1/4 to 1 cup (1.25 to 5 oz / 35 to 142 g) raisins, depending on sugar sensitivity

4 eggs (7 oz / 198 g)

3/4 cup (6 oz / 170 g) unsweetened soy milk or other milk

1/4 cup (2 oz / 57 g) salted butter or margarine, melted

2 1/2 teaspoons vanilla extract

1/4 teaspoon liquid stevia

Cinnamon Swirl

1 1/4 cups Splenda, Stevia Extract in the Raw, ZSweet, or Truvia, or 1/2 cup plus 2 tablespoons New Roots Stevia Sugar

2 teaspoons ground cinnamon

2 tablespoons unsweetened soy milk or other milk

1/2 teaspoon vanilla extract

Preheat the oven to 350°F (177°C). Grease a Bundt pan entirely with butter or margarine (see page 167) and place it in the freezer.

In a medium bowl, combine the hazelnut flour, almond flour, Splenda, baking powder, salt, and cinnamon and whisk until well mixed. Stir in the raisins. In a large bowl, whisk the eggs, milk, butter, vanilla, and liquid stevia together. Add the flour mixture and stir with a large spoon for 1 to 2 minutes to make a thick, sticky batter (see page 27).

Remove your prepared pan from the freezer, then dust the entire inner surface with almond flour. Pour the mixture into the prepared pan and jiggle it to evenly distribute the batter into every nook and cranny.

To make the cinnamon swirl, combine all of the ingredients in a small bowl and whisk until thoroughly blended. Drizzle the mixture over the batter and use a small spatula or knife to swirl the slurry evenly across and halfway through the batter. Then, jiggle the pan to again evenly distribute the batter.

Bake for 30 minutes, then rotate and bake for 20 to 25 minutes, until golden brown and springy when pressed in the center and a toothpick inserted into the middle of the cake comes out clean.

Let the cake cool in the pan for 5 minutes before inverting it onto a serving platter or wire rack. Let it cool for 15 more minutes before carefully removing the pan, then let it cool for at least 20 more minutes before slicing and serving.

Applesauce Coffee Cake

MAKES 12 SERVINGS

This cake is like homemade apple pie and pound cake combined in one delicious coffee cake. We created this recipe using a typical unsweetened store brand of applesauce, with a very wet consistency that pours from the jar easily. If your applesauce is thick, as some organic brands tend to be, you will need to add water—as much as 1/4 or even 1/2 cup—so the batter consistency matches the description in the instructions. As with any recipe, the dough dictates what it needs, so use the descriptive cues to help with your adjustments. In this instance, the batter should be thick and sticky, like cooked oatmeal, but also easy to transfer into the pan with a large spoon or rubber spatula. If it seems overly stiff and moldable, like playdough, then it needs the additional water.

2 cups (8 oz / 227 g) almond flour, plus more for dusting the pan

2 cups (8 oz / 227 g) pecan flour (see page 12)

2 cups Splenda or Stevia Extract in the Raw, or 1 cup New Roots Stevia Sugar

1 1/2 teaspoons baking powder

1/4 teaspoon salt

1 teaspoon ground cinnamon

5 eggs (8.75 oz / 248 g)

1 cup (8.75 oz / 248 g) unsweetened applesauce (see headnote)

1/4 cup (2 oz / 57 g) salted butter or margarine, melted

2 teaspoons vanilla extract

Vanilla Glaze

1 cup Splenda or Stevia Extract in the Raw, or 1/2 cup New Roots Stevia Sugar

4 teaspoons unsweetened soy milk or other milk

1 teaspoon vanilla extract

Preheat the oven to 350°F (177°C). Grease a Bundt pan or tube pan entirely with butter or margarine (see page 167) and place it in the freezer.

In a medium bowl, combine the almond flour, pecan flour, sweetener, baking powder, salt, and cinnamon and whisk until well mixed. In a large bowl, whisk the eggs, applesauce, butter, and vanilla together until thoroughly blended. Add the flour mixture and stir with a large spoon for 1 to 2 minutes to make a thick, sticky batter (see page 27).

Remove your prepared pan from the freezer, then dust the entire inner surface with almond flour. Pour the mixture into the prepared pan and jiggle it to evenly distribute the batter into every nook and cranny. Bake for 30 minutes, then rotate and bake for about 30 more minutes, until springy when pressed in the center and a toothpick inserted into the middle of the cake comes out clean.

Let the cake cool in the pan for 20 minutes before turning it out onto a wire rack to cool completely.

Meanwhile, make the glaze. In a small bowl, combine all of the ingredients and whisk until thoroughly blended. The mixture should have a consistency similar to sour cream; if it's too thin, add more Splenda. Put the mixture in a piping bag or small plastic sandwich bag with one tiny corner snipped off. Pipe the glaze over the cooled cake in a squiggle pattern.

VARIATION

Applesauce-Coffee Coffee Cake: For a coffee cake infused with coffee flavor, add 1 to 2 tablespoons of instant coffee crystals when mixing the dry ingredients.

Orange-Spice Coffee Cake

MAKES 12 SERVINGS

The spices and orange extract in this coffee cake give it an exotic flavor some-what similar to a traditional fruitcake. Diet orange soda may seem like an unusual ingredient—and it is!—but it adds more orange flavor without adding the sugars naturally present in orange juice. If sugar isn't an issue, simply substitute the fresh juice from the tangerines or oranges used to make the zest.

2 cups (8 oz / 227 g) pecan flour (see page 12)

2 cups (8 oz / 227 g) almond flour, plus more for dusting the pan

1 1/2 cups Splenda or Stevia Extract in the Raw, or 3/4 cup New Roots Stevia Sugar

2 teaspoons baking powder

1/2 teaspoon salt

2 teaspoons ground cinnamon

1/2 teaspoon ground nutmeg

1/2 teaspoon ground allspice

1/2 teaspoon ground ginger

1/4 teaspoon ground cloves

1/2 cup (1.75 oz / 50 g) pecans, lightly toasted (see Tip, page 172) and chopped

5 eggs (8.75 oz / 248 g)

1 cup (8 oz / 227 g) diet orange soda or fresh orange or tangerine juice

1/2 cup (4 oz / 113 g) salted butter or margarine, melted

1 teaspoon fresh lemon juice

1 teaspoon orange extract

1 tablespoon grated tangerine or orange zest

Pecan Topping

1/2 cup (1.75 oz / 50 g) pecans, lightly toasted (see Tip, page 172) and chopped

1/4 cup Splenda, Stevia Extract in the Raw, ZSweet, or Truvia, or 2 tablespoons New Roots Stevia Sugar

Preheat the oven to 350°F (177°C). Grease a Bundt pan entirely with butter or margarine (see page 167) and place it in the freezer.

In a medium bowl, combine the pecan flour, almond flour, sweetener, baking powder, salt, cinnamon, nutmeg, allspice, ginger, and cloves. Whisk until well mixed. Stir in the pecans. In a large bowl, whisk the eggs, soda, butter, lemon juice, orange extract, and zest together until thoroughly blended. Add the flour mixture and stir with a large spoon for 1 to 2 minutes to make a thick, sticky batter (see page 27).

Remove your prepared pan from the freezer, then dust the entire inner surface with almond flour. Pour the batter into the prepared pan and jiggle it to evenly distribute the batter into every nook and cranny.

To make the topping, combine all of the ingredients in a small bowl and stir until thoroughly mixed. Sprinkle the topping evenly over the batter.

Bake for 30 minutes, then rotate and bake for about 30 more minutes, until golden brown and springy when pressed in the center and a toothpick inserted into the middle of the cake comes out clean.

Let the cake cool in the pan for about 20 minutes before inverting it onto a serving platter or wire rack. Let it cool for at least 10 more minutes before slicing and serving. You can serve the cake topping side up or topping side down.

Hazelnut-Almond Coffee Cake

MAKES 12 TO 14 SERVINGS

Though seemingly similar to our Hazelnut-Coconut Coffee Cake (page 173), this variation replaces some of the hazelnut flour with almond flour, and gets its coconut flavor from coconut flakes, not coconut milk. These subtle changes create a totally different final product. This cake is a great choice for birthdays and other celebrations, or for dessert after a special meal, especially if garnished with fresh berries and Sugar-Free Whipped Cream (page 202).

2 cups (8 oz / 227 g) hazelnut flour

1 cup (4 oz / 113 g) almond flour

1¹/₂ cups Splenda or Stevia Extract in the Raw, or ³/₄ cup New Roots Stevia Sugar

1 tablespoon baking powder

¹/₂ teaspoon xanthan gum

³/₄ cup (5.75 oz / 163 g) almonds, lightly toasted (see Tip, page 172) and chopped

¹/₂ cup (1.25 oz / 35 g) unsweetened coconut flakes, toasted (see Tip, page 150)

4 eggs (7 oz / 198 g)

1 cup (8 oz / 227 g) unsweetened soy milk or other milk

¹/₄ cup (2 oz / 57 g) salted butter or margarine, melted

1¹/₂ teaspoons vanilla

1¹/₄ teaspoons liquid stevia

Cream Cheese Frosting (page 184)

Preheat the oven to 375°F (191°C). Grease a Bundt pan entirely with butter or margarine (see page 167) and place it in the freezer.

In a medium bowl, combine the hazelnut flour, almond flour, Splenda, baking powder, and xanthan gum and whisk until well mixed. Stir in the almonds and coconut flakes. In a large bowl, whisk the eggs, milk, butter, vanilla, and liquid stevia together until thoroughly blended. Add the flour mixture and stir with a large spoon for 1 to 2 minutes to make a thick, sticky batter (see page 27).

Remove your prepared pan from the freezer, then dust the entire inner surface with almond, pecan, or coconut flour. Pour the mixture into the prepared pan and jiggle it to evenly distribute the batter into every nook and cranny. Bake for 30 minutes, then gently rotate and bake for about 30 more minutes, until golden brown and springy when pressed in the center and a toothpick inserted into the middle of the cake comes out clean.

Let the cake cool in the pan for at least for 20 minutes before turning it out onto a wire rack to cool completely.

To frost the cake, spread some frosting over the top, spreading it to an even thickness, then spread the remaining frosting over the entire cake.

Chocolate Cream Cheese Cake

MAKES 10 TO 12 SERVINGS

This moist and delicious cake isn't technically a cheesecake; rather, it's a cake with cream cheese in the batter. Did we also mention the word "chocolate"? Of course, the perfect accompaniment would be sugar-free ice cream or frozen yogurt or a dollop of Sugar-Free Whipped Cream (page 202). Another fun serving suggestion is to drizzle sugar-free chocolate syrup over the top of individual slices, then sprinkle with toasted, chopped nuts.

2 cups (8 oz / 227 g) hazelnut flour

2 cups (8 oz / 227 g) almond flour

2¹/₂ cups Splenda or Stevia Extract in the Raw, or 1¹/₄ cups New Roots Stevia Sugar

³/₄ cup (2.25 oz / 64 g) unsweetened natural cocoa powder (not Dutch-process)

2 teaspoons baking powder

¹/₂ teaspoon salt

5 eggs (8.75 oz / 248 g)

8 ounces (227 g) cream cheese, at room temperature

³/₄ cup (6 oz / 170 g) salted butter or margarine, melted

2 teaspoons vanilla extract

1¹/₂ teaspoons liquid stevia

Preheat the oven to 375°F (191°C). Grease a Bundt pan entirely with butter or margarine (see page 167) and place it in the freezer.

In a medium bowl, combine the hazelnut flour, almond flour, Splenda, cocoa powder, baking powder, and salt and whisk until well mixed. In the bowl of an electric mixer or a large bowl, combine the eggs, cream cheese, butter, vanilla, and liquid stevia and mix with the paddle attachment at medium-low speed or stir vigorously with a large spoon for 1 minute. Add the flour mixture and mix at medium-low speed or stir vigorously with a large spoon for about 1 minute to make a smooth, thick, pourable batter (see page 27).

Remove your prepared pan from the freezer, then dust the entire inner surface with almond, pecan, or coconut flour. Pour the mixture into the prepared pan and jiggle it to evenly distribute the batter into every nook and cranny. Bake for 30 minutes, then gently rotate and bake for 20 to 30 minutes, until the cake is springy when pressed in the center and a toothpick inserted into the middle of the cake comes out clean.

Let the cake cool in the pan for 20 minutes before turning it out onto a wire rack. Let cool for at least 20 more minutes before slicing and serving.

Carrot Cake with Cream Cheese Frosting

Everyone loves carrot cake, but if you can't eat wheat or sugar, you may think it isn't an option—especially because carrots have a relatively high carb content. In this recipe, the fiber in the coconut and pecan flour helps keep the glycemic load low. Because this recipe calls for so many egg whites, we recommend that you purchase liquid egg whites so you don't have a quandary about what to do with all of the yolks. To use liquid egg whites, simply weigh out the amount specified in the recipe. Also, note that the cream cheese frosting is optional (but highly recommended!).

1 cup (4 oz / 113 g) coconut flour (see Tip, page 14)

1 cup (4 oz / 113 g) pecan flour (see page 12)

1/4 cup (0.75 oz / 21 g) unsweetened shredded dried coconut, lightly toasted (see Tip, page 150)

2 cups Splenda or Stevia Extract in the Raw, or 1 cup New Roots Stevia Sugar

2 teaspoons baking powder

1 1/4 teaspoons salt

1 1/2 teaspoons ground cinnamon

8 egg whites (10 oz / 284 g) or 6 eggs (10.5 oz / 298 g)

1 1/4 cup (10 oz / 284 g) unsweetened soy milk or other milk

1/2 cup (4 oz / 113 g) salted butter or margarine, melted

2 teaspoons vanilla extract

1/4 teaspoon liquid stevia

2 1/2 cups (12 oz / 340 g) packed finely shredded carrots

Cream Cheese Frosting

1 1/2 pounds (680 g) cream cheese, at room temperature

1/2 cup (4 oz / 113 g) salted butter or margarine, at room temperature

1 cup Splenda or Stevia Extract in the Raw, or 1/2 cup New Roots Stevia Sugar

1/2 teaspoon ground cinnamon

4 teaspoons vanilla extract

1 tablespoon unsweetened soy milk or other milk

1/8 teaspoon liquid stevia

Pecans or other nuts, toasted (see Tip, page 172) and chopped, for garnish (optional)

Unsweetened coconut flakes, toasted (see Tip, page 150), for garnish (optional)

Preheat the oven to 325°F (163°C). Line the bottom of two 8-inch round cake pans with parchment paper, then mist the inside walls of the pans along with the parchment with spray oil.   (CONTINUED)

In a medium bowl, combine the coconut flour, pecan flour, shredded coconut, Splenda, baking powder, salt, and cinnamon and whisk until well mixed. In a large bowl, whisk the egg whites, milk, butter, vanilla, and liquid stevia together until thoroughly blended. Stir in the carrots. Add the flour mixture and stir with a large spoon for 1 to 2 minutes to make a thick, sticky batter (see page 27). If the batter is too thick to pour, add a little more milk.

Pour the batter into the prepared pans. Use a spatula to evenly spread the batter, or jiggle the pan to evenly distribute the batter in the pan. Bake for 35 minutes, then switch racks and bake for about 30 more minutes, until the cakes are lightly golden and springy when pressed in the center and a toothpick inserted into the middle of each cake comes out clean.

Let the cakes cool in the pans for at least 20 minutes.

Meanwhile, make the frosting. In the bowl of an electric mixer or a large bowl, combine all of the ingredients and mix with the paddle attachment on medium speed or stir vigorously with a large spoon until thoroughly blended. If using an electric mixer, switch to the whisk attachment and mix at medium-high speed for about 3 minutes, until the mixture

is fluffy and very creamy; if mixing by hand, switch to a sturdy whisk and beat vigorously.

As the cakes cool, they should shrink from the pan walls; if not, run an icing spatula or a thin knife around the edges. Invert the cakes onto two plates. They can be eaten as they are or be frosted, either singly or as a two-layer cake. For a two-layer cake, spread some frosting over the top of the lower layer, spreading it to an even thickness of about ¼ inch. Position the second layer on top and then spread the remaining frosting over the entire cake. Sprinkle the pecans, coconut, or both over the top and/or sides of the cake if you like. Keep refrigerated.

Lemon and Poppy Seed Cake

MAKES 10 TO 12 SERVINGS

A refreshing, buttery, lemony treat, this cake has a creamy texture and is excellent served with a scoop of sugar-free lemon sorbet or a dollop of Sugar-Free Whipped Cream (page 202). One important note: Don't try to substitute vegetable oil for the butter or margarine in this recipe. It just won't create the same flavor synergy with the lemon juice that you'll get from butter or a good-quality buttery spread.

3 cups (12 oz / 340 g) almond flour

1 cup (4 oz / 113 g) hazelnut flour

2¹/₂ cups Splenda or Stevia Extract in the Raw, or 1¹/₄ cups New Roots Stevia Sugar

2 teaspoons poppy seeds, or more as desired

1¹/₂ teaspoons baking powder

5 eggs (8.75 oz / 248 g)

1 cup (8 oz / 227 g) salted butter or margarine, melted

³/₄ cup (6 oz / 170 g) fresh lemon juice

2 teaspoons vanilla extract

¹/₂ teaspoon liquid stevia

Preheat the oven to 350°F (177°C). Grease a Bundt pan entirely with butter or margarine (see page 167) and place it in the freezer.

In a medium bowl, combine the almond flour, hazelnut flour, Splenda, poppy seeds, and baking powder and whisk until well mixed. In a large bowl, whisk the eggs, butter, lemon juice, vanilla, and liquid stevia together until thoroughly blended. Add the flour mixture and stir with a large spoon for 1 to 2 minutes to make a thick, sticky batter (see page 27).

Remove your prepared pan from the freezer, then dust the entire inner surface with almond or hazelnut flour. Pour the mixture into the prepared pan and jiggle it to evenly distribute the batter into every nook and cranny. Bake for 30 minutes, then gently rotate and bake for about 25 minutes, until firm and springy when pressed in the center and a toothpick inserted into the middle of the cake comes out clean.

Let the cake cool in the pan for 20 minutes before turning it out onto a wire rack. Let cool for at least 20 more minutes before slicing and serving.

Homestyle Pound Cake

MAKES 12 TO 14 SERVINGS

Pound cake earned its name because recipes for traditional versions include a pound each of flour, butter, eggs, and sugar. Most modern versions use different amounts of those ingredients, and of course this version doesn't use a pound of sugar! Nonetheless, it is a sweet and buttery, wonderfully dense multipurpose treat with a flavor akin to pound cake. Although we generally encourage you to play with the nut and seed flours to create your own variations, in this recipe the almond flour is primary and should not be replaced. However, you can substitute pecan, walnut, or additional almond flour for the hazelnut flour, though we love the hazelnut version. It's great topped with Sugar-Free Whipped Cream (page 202). Or, for a sensational dessert, drizzle sugar-free yogurt over the cake, then top each slice with a few dollops of sugar-free fruit preserves.

3 cups (12 oz / 340 g) almond flour, plus more for dusting the pan

1 cup (4 oz / 113 g) hazelnut flour

2 cups Splenda or Stevia Extract in the Raw, or 1 cup New Roots Stevia Sugar

1¹/2 teaspoons baking powder

¹/4 teaspoon salt

¹/2 teaspoon ground nutmeg, allspice, cinnamon, or a combination

5 eggs (8.75 oz / 248 g)

³/4 cup (6 oz / 170 g) salted butter or margarine, melted

¹/2 cup (4 oz / 113 g) unsweetened soy milk or other milk

1 tablespoon vanilla extract

¹/4 teaspoon liquid stevia

Preheat the oven to 350°F (177°C). Mist the bottom and sides of a 5 by 9-inch loaf pan with spray oil, then line the bottom of the loaf pan with parchment and mist it again with the spray oil.

In a medium bowl, combine the almond flour, hazelnut flour, Splenda, baking powder, salt, and nutmeg and whisk until well mixed. In a large bowl, whisk the eggs, butter, milk, vanilla, and liquid stevia together until thoroughly blended. Add the flour mixture and stir with a large spoon for 1 to 2 minutes to make a smooth, sticky, pourable batter (see page 27).

Pour the mixture into the prepared pan; it should be no more than three-quarters full. Bake for 30 minutes, then gently rotate and bake for about 30 more minutes, until golden and springy when pressed in the center and a toothpick inserted into the middle of the cake comes out clean.

Let the cake cool in the pan for 20 minutes before turning it out onto a wire rack. Let cool for at least 20 more minutes before slicing and serving.

Pound Cake with Crumb Topping

MAKES 12 TO 14 SERVINGS

Once you've mastered the Homestyle Pound Cake, opposite, add some texture and flavor with this twist.

1 batch unbaked Homestyle Pound Cake batter (page 188)

Crumb Topping
1 cup (4 oz / 113 g) almond flour
1 cup Splenda or Stevia Extract in the Raw, or 1/2 cup New Roots Stevia Sugar

1/8 teaspoon salt
1/2 teaspoon ground cinnamon
1/8 teaspoon ground nutmeg, cloves, allspice, cinnamon, cardamom, or ginger
1/2 cup (4 oz / 113 g) salted butter or margarine, melted

Preheat the oven to 350°F (177°C). Mist the bottom and sides of a 5 by 9-inch loaf pan with spray oil, then line the bottom of the loaf pan with baking parchment and mist it again with the spray oil. Have the cake batter ready.

To make the topping, combine the almond flour, sweetener, salt, cinnamon, and nutmeg in a medium bowl and whisk until well mixed. Whisk in the butter to make a lumpy dough, then use your fingers to break the lumps into crumbles. If the crumbles are bigger than you'd like, put the mixture in the refrigerator for 10 minutes, then crumble it into smaller bits.

Pour half of the batter into the prepared pan and spread it into a smooth layer with a rubber spatula (or jiggle the pan). Sprinkle half of the topping evenly over the surface. Pour in the remaining batter and gently spread it into a smooth layer, as above, then sprinkle the remaining topping evenly over the surface.

Bake for 30 minutes, then gently rotate and bake for about 30 more minutes, until the crumbs are golden brown and a toothpick inserted into the middle of the cake comes out clean.

Let the cake cool in the pan for 20 minutes before turning it out onto a wire rack. Let cool for at least 20 more minutes before slicing and serving.

Sweet Pecan Bread

MAKES 10 TO 12 SERVINGS

This dessert can be baked as a coffee cake or sweet loaf bread, and it tastes like a pecan cinnamon roll! This bread can be baked in a loaf pan, but for a festive appearance, bake it in a Bundt pan. For a glaze, you can use the Hot Cross Buns glaze topping (page 57), or dust with powdered erythritol (see page 148). For those who are not counting their carbs, you can add 1/2 cup of raisins to the batter with the dry ingredients.

2 cups (8 oz / 227 g) pecan flour

1 cup (4 oz / 113 g) almond flour, plus more for dusting the pan

1 1/2 cups Splenda or Stevia Extract in the Raw, or 3/4 cup New Roots Stevia Sugar

3/4 cup (2.75 oz / 78 g) chopped pecans

4 teaspoons baking powder

2 teaspoons ground cinnamon

1/2 teaspoon salt

1/2 teaspoon xanthan gum

4 eggs (7 oz / 198 g)

1 cup (8 oz / 227 g) unsweetened soy milk or other milk

1/4 cup (2 oz / 57 g) butter or butter substitute, melted

1 1/4 teaspoons liquid stevia

1 1/2 teaspoons vanilla extract

Preheat the oven to 375°F (191°C). Grease a Bundt pan or mini Bundt pans with butter or margarine (see page 167) and place it in the freezer.

In a medium bowl combine the pecan flour, almond flour, Splenda, chopped pecans, baking powder, ground cinnamon, salt, and xanthan gum and whisk until well blended. In a large bowl, whisk the eggs, milk, butter, liquid stevia, and vanilla together. Add the flour mixture and stir with a large spoon for 1 to 2 minutes to make a thick, sticky batter (see page 27).

Remove your prepared pan from the freezer, then dust the entire inner surface with almond flour. Pour the mixture into the prepared pan and smooth the top with a rubber spatula. Jiggle the pan to evenly distribute the batter into every nook and cranny. If making mini Bundt cakes, fill each cup three-fourths full. For a full-size Bundt cake, bake for 30 minutes, then rotate and bake for an additional 20 to 30 minutes, or until the bread is golden brown and springy when pressed in the center and a toothpick inserted into the middle comes out clean. For mini Bundt cakes, cut the baking time in half and follow the doneness cues above.

Let the cake cool in the pan for 5 minutes before inverting it onto a serving platter or wire rack. Let it cool for another 15 minutes before carefully removing the pan. Cool for another 10 to 20 minutes before slicing and serving.

Chapter Seven

PIES

Once you have a good crust, you can make a wide variety of pies. This chapter provides a recipe for an excellent, all-purpose gluten-free sugar-free crust, along with two variations. These crusts are very versatile. They're great for fruit pies, pumpkin pie, and pecan pie, and you'll find recipes for all of those fillings in this chapter. Or you can prebake them and use a precooked filling, as in the Vanilla Cream Pie (page 202) and its variations. To up the ante, we've even included a recipe for a chocolate crust. For a truly special dessert that will grace any festive table, try using the chocolate crust for pecan pie or any of the cream pies. Here are a few tips on the pie recipes in this chapter:

- Because various brands of nut flour, levels of grind, and types of nuts absorb liquid differently, you may need to adjust these recipes. If you find that your piecrust dough is more dry and crumbly than described, feel free to add more milk until it becomes pressable.

- Use a glass pie pan so you can see the bottom of the crust to make sure it isn't overbrowning.

- Fruit pies are tricky for people with diabetes or anyone counting carbs because fruit has natural sugar. Luckily, it's also full of fiber, which helps lower its glycemic index. These recipes were specifically created with diabetics in mind, so that everyone can enjoy a slice of pie.

- Happily, the pie fillings in this chapter are vegan-friendly and can be made with powdered egg replacer.

- We recommend cutting these pies into 8 to 10 slices. That yields a reasonable serving size that most people can enjoy regardless of dietary restrictions.

- Store leftover pie in an airtight container in the refrigerator.

Chocolate Piecrust

MAKES ONE 10-INCH PIECRUST

This piecrust is a great choice for cream pies, especially Chocolate Cream Pie (page 204). Who says you can't have chocolate on chocolate?

1 cup (4 oz / 113 g) almond flour

1 cup (4 oz / 113 g) coconut flour (see Tip, page 14)

1/4 cup Splenda or Stevia Extract in the Raw, or 2 tablespoons New Roots Stevia Sugar

1/4 cup (0.75 oz / 21 g) unsweetened natural cocoa powder (not Dutch-process)

1/2 teaspoon baking power

1/4 cup (2 oz / 57 g) salted butter or margarine, melted

6 tablespoons unsweetened chocolate soy milk or other milk

1 tablespoon vanilla extract

1/8 teaspoon liquid stevia

If you'll be baking the crust before filling it, preheat the oven to 325°F (163°C). Lightly mist a 9- or 10-inch pie pan with spray oil.

In a large bowl, combine the almond flour, coconut flour, Splenda, cocoa powder, and baking powder and whisk until well mixed. Add the butter, milk, vanilla, and liquid stevia and stir with a large spoon for 1 to 2 minutes. The dough will be stiff and playdough-like (see page 27).

Put the dough in the prepared pan and lightly mist the top with spray oil. Spread the dough with your fingers, pressing it in an even layer to line the pan. Prick the bottom and sides with a fork to help prevent bubbles and air pockets. If you'll be filling the pie before baking it, it's ready to go.

If prebaking the crust, cover the edges with aluminum foil, then bake for 10 minutes. Rotate the pan and bake for 7 more minutes, then remove the foil and bake for 3 to 5 minutes, or until the crust is crisp and firm to the touch.

Almond-Pecan Piecrust

MAKES ONE 10-INCH PIECRUST

Here's our favorite piecrust. It's a flaky treat that you might be tempted to eat like shortbread cookies (and who are we to stop you if you want to do that?). The two variations below are close contenders; the only difference is substituting hazelnut flour or coconut flour for the pecan flour. Once you've mastered this recipe, or one of its variations, use it as a template for creating your own versions. When deciding which flours to use, consider how their flavors will work with the filling. Beyond the sweet fillings included in this chapter, you can also use these crusts for quiches and other savory pies. Enjoy!

1 cup (4 oz / 113 g) almond flour

1 cup (4 oz / 113 g) pecan flour (see page 12)

1/4 cup Splenda or Stevia Extract in the Raw, or 2 tablespoons New Roots Stevia Sugar

1/2 teaspoon baking powder

1/4 cup (2 oz / 57 g) salted butter or margarine, melted

3 tablespoons unsweetened soy milk or other milk

1 1/2 teaspoons vanilla extract

If you'll be baking the crust before filling it, preheat the oven to 325°F (163°C). Lightly mist a 9- or 10-inch pie pan with spray oil.

In a large bowl, combine the almond flour, pecan flour, sweetener, and baking powder and whisk until well mixed. Add the butter, milk, and vanilla and stir with a large spoon for 1 to 2 minutes. The dough will be stiff and playdough-like (see page 27).

Put the dough in the prepared pan and lightly mist the top of the dough with spray oil. Spread the dough with your fingers, pressing it in an even layer to line the pan. Prick the bottom and sides with a fork to help prevent bubbles and air pockets. If you'll be filling the pie before baking it, it's ready to go.

If prebaking the crust, cover the edges with aluminum foil, then bake for 10 minutes. Rotate the pan and bake for 7 minutes, then remove the foil and bake an additional 3 to 5 minutes, until the dough is firm to the touch and just starting to brown.

VARIATIONS

Almond-Hazelnut Piecrust: Substitute hazelnut flour for the pecan flour.

Almond-Coconut Piecrust: Substitute coconut flour for the pecan flour. Denene loves this one and believes that this is the most versatile piecrust of them all.

Maple-Pecan Pie

MAKES ENOUGH FILLING FOR 1 PIE

This pie, which features the wonderful flavor combination of pecans and maple, is always a hit. Do not chop the pecans too small. It's best to have a mix of large and medium-size pieces, which tend to float to the top of the pie, whereas finely chopped pieces usually sink. For those who can't eat sugar, this is a very special treat—even more so with a scoop of sugar-free vanilla ice cream on top!

1 unbaked piecrust (use any of the recipes or variations on pages 194 and 196)

3 eggs (5.25 oz / 149 g)

1 cup (8 oz / 227 g) sugar-free maple-flavored syrup (see page 22)

5 tablespoons (2.5 oz / 71 g) salted butter or margarine, melted

2 teaspoons vanilla extract

1/2 teaspoon liquid stevia

1 cup Splenda or Stevia Extract in the Raw, or 1/2 cup New Roots Stevia Sugar

2 cups (7 oz / 198 g) pecans, coarsely chopped

Preheat the oven to 350°F (177°C). Have the piecrust ready.

In a large bowl, whisk the eggs, sugar-free maple-flavored syrup, butter, vanilla, and liquid stevia together until thoroughly blended. Add the Splenda and whisk gently just until well blended; don't whisk so much that the mixture gets foamy. Fold in the pecans.

Put the crust on a baking sheet and pour the filling in. Cover the edges of the crust with foil to prevent burning. Bake for 30 minutes, then carefully rotate the baking sheet and bake for about 25 more minutes. Remove the foil and bake for about 5 more minutes, until the center of the pie is set and springs back slightly when pressed gently and a knife inserted into the middle of the pie comes out clean.

Let the pie cool for at least 1 hour before slicing and serving. Keep refrigerated.

Apple Crumble Pie

MAKES ENOUGH FILLING AND TOPPING FOR 1 PIE

There is nothing like a good old-fashioned apple crumble pie, so we wanted to create a gluten-free, sugar-free version for this book. You can use any type of apples, but in our opinion slightly tart varieties with low a glycemic load, such as Granny Smith or pippins, yield the best results. Denene has found that Fuji apples, for example, contain too much sugar for some diabetics. You can peel the apples if you like, but we recommend leaving the peel on for added nutrients and fiber. This pie is delicious on its own, but even better with sugar-free vanilla ice cream.

1 unbaked piecrust (use any of the recipes or variations on pages 194 and 196)

Crumble Topping

$3/4$ cup (3 oz / 85 g) almond flour

$1/4$ cup Splenda, Stevia Extract in the Raw, Truvia, or Zsweet, or 2 tablespoons New Roots Stevia sugar

$1/2$ teaspoon ground cinnamon

$1/4$ teaspoon ground ginger

$1/4$ cup (2 oz / 57 g) salted butter or margarine, melted

1 teaspoon vanilla extract

Apple Filling

5 cups (28 oz / 794 g) thinly sliced apples (about $1/4$ inch thick)

1 cup Splenda or Stevia Extract in the Raw, or $1/2$ cup New Roots Stevia Sugar

$1/4$ cup (1 oz / 28 g) almond flour

$1 1/2$ teaspoons ground cinnamon

2 tablespoons salted butter or margarine, melted

1 teaspoon fresh lemon juice

$1/2$ teaspoon liquid stevia

Preheat the oven to 375°F (191°C). Have the piecrust ready.

To make the topping, put all of the ingredients in a small bowl and stir with a large spoon or rubber spatula until thoroughly combined. The mixture should be crumbly and dry. If it lumps up rather than forming crumbles, refrigerate for about 30 minutes, until hardened, and then crumble it with your fingers.

To make the filling, put the apples in a large bowl. In a separate bowl, combine the Splenda, almond flour, cinnamon, butter, lemon juice, and liquid stevia and stir gently with a large spoon or rubber spatula until thoroughly combined. Add this mixture to the apples and mix together until all the apples are thoroughly coated. Then pour the mixture, juices and all, into the unbaked piecrust; the apples will mound up higher than the edges of the pan.

Sprinkle the crumble topping evenly over the apples.   (CONTINUED)

Put the pie on a baking sheet and cover the edges of the crust with foil to prevent burning. Bake for 20 minutes, then rotate the baking sheet and bake for about 20 more minutes. Remove the foil from the edges of the piecrust and bake for about 10 minutes, until the topping and crust are golden brown.

Let the pie cool for at least 1 hour before slicing and serving. Keep refrigerated.

VARIATION

Double-Crust Apple Pie: For a double-crusted pie, forgo the crumble topping. Instead, prepare and roll out a second piecrust as described below, place it over the top of the filled pie, and flute the edges to seal it to the lower crust. Be sure to cut a couple of steam vents in the top before baking. Alternatively, you can cut the second crust into strips and make a lattice crust on top. Bake until the crust is golden brown.

Tip: Rolling Out a Top Crust

You can roll out piecrust to make a top crust, or cut it into strips to make a lattice crust. The technique is similar to rolling out crackers: Form the dough into a ball. Mist 2 pieces of parchment paper or 2 silicone mats with spray oil. Place the dough between the oiled surfaces, press down to flatten somewhat, then use a rolling pin to roll and flatten the dough until slightly thinner than 1/4 inch.

Lay the rolled out crust over the filled pie, then trim the edges and crimp the top crust to the bottom crust. Or, cut the rolled out crust into 1 inch strips and weave a lattice over the top of a filled pie; trim the edges.

Pumpkin Pie

The winter holidays just wouldn't be the same without pumpkin pie. Here's a version everyone can enjoy, regardless of sensitivity to gluten or sugar. Plus, it can be made in advance—always a bonus during the busy holiday season. It keeps well in the refrigerator for 3 or 4 days, and in the freezer for weeks. Don't forget the Sugar-Free Whipped Cream (page 202) or ice cream!

1 unbaked piecrust (use any of the recipes or variations on page 194 and 196)

3 eggs (5.25 oz / 149 g)

1 can (15 oz / 425 g) unsweetened pumpkin puree

1 cup (8 oz / 227 g) unsweetened soy milk or other milk

1 cup Splenda or Stevia Extract in the Raw, or 1/2 cup New Roots Stevia Sugar

1 teaspoon ground cinnamon

1/2 teaspoon ground ginger

1/2 teaspoon ground allspice, or 1/4 teaspoon ground cloves

11/2 teaspoons vanilla extract

3/4 teaspoon liquid stevia

Preheat the oven to 375°F (191°C). Have the piecrust ready.

In a large bowl, whisk the eggs. Add the pumpkin, milk, Splenda, cinnamon, ginger, allspice, vanilla, and liquid stevia and whisk to make a smooth, pourable batter.

Put the crust on a baking sheet and pour the filling in. Cover the edges of the crust with foil to prevent burning. Bake for 25 minutes, then rotate the baking sheet and bake for about 25 minutes, until the center of the pie is slightly springy to the touch. Remove the foil and bake for about 10 minutes, until the edges of the crust are golden brown and a knife or toothpick inserted into the middle of the pie comes out clean.

Let the pie cool for at least 1 hour before slicing and serving. Keep refrigerated.

Vanilla Cream Pie

MAKES ENOUGH FILLING FOR 1 PIE

In essence, a cream pie is basically a prebaked pie crust filled with pastry cream, a custard made with two thickeners: eggs, which are the defining ingredient of all custards, and some sort of starch—usually cornstarch or arrowroot powder. This second thickener is what distinguishes pastry cream from baked custards such as flan or crème brûlée. Because we aren't using starches in any of our recipes, making a satisfying pastry cream was a challenge, but after a great deal of experimentation, Denene developed this recipe, which is thickened with gelatin or, for vegetarians, agar.

1 baked piecrust (use any of the recipes or variations on pages 194 and 196)

2 cups (16 oz / 454 g) unsweetened soy milk or other milk

$1/2$ cup Splenda or Stevia Extract in the Raw, or $1/4$ cup New Roots Stevia Sugar

3 eggs (5.25 oz / 149 g)

$1/4$ cup (1 oz / 28 g) almond flour

$1/4$ cup (2 oz / 57 g) salted butter or margarine

1 tablespoon vanilla extract

$1/4$ teaspoon liquid stevia

$1 1/2$ packets or $3 1/4$ teaspoons (0.375 oz / 10.5 g) unflavored powdered gelatin, or $3 1/4$ teaspoons agar powder

Sugar-Free Whipped Cream

1 cup (8 oz / 227 g) cold whipping cream

$1/2$ to 1 teaspoon vanilla extract (optional)

10 to 15 drops liquid stevia

Have the piecrust ready. In a heavy sauce pan, combine the milk and half of the Splenda and cook over medium-high heat until almost simmering.

Meanwhile, combine the eggs, the remaining Splenda, and the almond flour and whisk until thoroughly blended. Ladle about one-fourth of the hot milk mixture into the egg mixture and whisk to combine. Then, ladle in another one-fourth of the hot milk and whisk to combine; this will gradually heat the eggs without curdling them.

Lower the heat to medium, pour in the egg mixture, and whisk until thoroughly blended. Switch to a wooden spoon and cook, stirring slowly and constantly to prevent burning and keep the eggs from curdling. As soon as the mixture is nearly simmering, with steady but gentle bubbling throughout, remove from the heat. The mixture will thicken slightly, but not as much as a traditional pastry cream; it will be more like gravy. Add the butter, vanilla, and liquid stevia and whisk gently until the butter melts and disappears into the mixture. If the mixture seems grainy or lumpy, whisk until smooth. If it curdles, don't worry, just whisk out the lumps as best you can.   (CONTINUED)

Let the mixture cool until you can touch the outside of the pot for more than 5 seconds. Sprinkle in the gelatin and whisk to distribute it evenly. It won't dissolve completely at first, but as the custard cools the gelatin will soften and begin to firm up the custard. Place a piece of plastic wrap tightly over the top of the saucepan to prevent the custard from forming a skin. After about 30 minutes, when the custard is just slightly warm to the touch, put it in the refrigerator until completely cooled. Remove it from the refrigerator and whisk or use an electric hand mixer to whip the filling until it becomes fluffy, about 1 to 2 minutes. Pour it into the prebaked pie shell, spreading it in an even layer. Mist the surface with spray oil, then cover with plastic wrap and refrigerate until thoroughly chilled, about 2 hours.

Just before serving the pie, make the whipped cream. Put the cold cream in a medium-size stainless steel bowl. Using an electric mixer with the whisk attachment at medium speed (or a strong arm with a sturdy whisk—and good endurance), beat the cream just until it begins to thicken. Add the vanilla and 10 drops of the liquid stevia and continue beating until soft to medium-firm peaks form. Avoid overbeating, or you'll make butter! Taste for sweetness. If you prefer it sweeter, gently whisk in more stevia, a drop at a time. (Store any unused whipped cream in the refrigerator in an airtight container; after a few days, it will begin to weep out some of the liquid, but you can simply rewhip it if that happens.)

Garnish the pie with the whipped cream and serve right away.

VARIATIONS

Coconut Cream Pie: Lightly toast ¾ cup (2.25 oz / 64 g) of unsweetened shredded dried coconut (see Tip, page 150). Reserve 2 tablespoons of the coconut and whisk the rest into the custard after it cools; in addition to providing texture, flavor, and fiber, this will fluff up the custard nicely. Proceed as directed in the recipe. After you garnish the pie with whipped cream, sprinkle the reserved coconut evenly over the top.

Chocolate Cream Pie: Increase the amount of Splenda or Stevia Extract in the Raw to 1 cup and add ¼ cup (0.75 oz / 21 g) of unsweetened natural cocoa powder when initially whisking the egg mixture. Sprinkle in an additional half packet of gelatin (0.125 oz / 3.5 g), for 2 packets total. Proceed as directed in the recipe. Or, add 4 ounces (112 g) of sugar-free semi-sweet chocolate (instead of the cocoa powder) when initially heating the milk, stirring it in once it's melted; in this case, don't increase the amount of Splenda or Stevia Extract in the Raw.

Banana Cream Pie: Mash 2 bananas and stir them into the custard as soon as you remove it from the heat, then add the gelatin. Slice a third banana crosswise into rounds and line the baked pie crust with the slices. Pour the warm custard over and proceed as directed.

Berry or Cherry Pie

MAKES ENOUGH FILLING FOR ONE 1 PIE

The amount of liquid stevia for this recipe will vary depending on the type of fruit you use: sour cherries are obviously less sweet than blueberries, and raspberries fall somewhere in the middle. With sweeter berries, it may be possible to omit the stevia altogether. Use ¼ teaspoon of liquid stevia for moderately sweet fruit, and up to 1 teaspoon for tart cherries.

1 unbaked piecrust (use any of the recipes or variations on pages 194 and 196)

2 egg whites (2.5 oz / 71 g)

½ cup Splenda or Stevia Extract in the Raw, or ¼ cup New Roots Stevia Sugar

4 cups fresh blueberries, raspberries, or other berries, or pitted sour cherries, fresh or canned (fully drained)

Up to 1 teaspoon liquid stevia, depending on the sweetness of the fruit

Preheat the oven to 375°F (191°C). Have the piecrust ready.

Put the egg whites in a large bowl. Using an electric mixer with the whisk attachment at medium-high speed (or a strong arm with a sturdy whisk—and good endurance), beat the eggs for 3 to 5 minutes, until fairly stiff peaks form. (This will go more quickly if the egg whites are at room temperature, rather than cold.) Add the Splenda and beat until it's evenly distributed and beginning to dissolve and stiff peaks form. Fold in the fruit and liquid stevia with a rubber spatula.

Put the crust on a baking sheet and pour the filling in. Cover the edges of the crust with aluminum foil and bake for 25 minutes, then rotate the baking sheet and bake for 20 more minutes. Remove the foil and bake for 5 to 10 more minutes, or until the crust is golden brown.

Let cool for at least 30 minutes before slicing and serving.

VARIATIONS

Berry Crumble Pie: Preheat the oven to 350°F (177°C). After pouring the filling into the crust, scatter Crumble Topping (page 199) over the fruit, then bake as directed, until the topping and crust are golden brown.

Double-Crust Berry Pie: For a double-crusted pie, preheat the oven to 350°F (177°C). Prepare and roll out a second piecrust as described in the Tip on page 200, place it over the top of the filled pie, and flute the edges to seal it to the lower crust. Be sure to cut a couple of steam vents in the top before baking. Alternatively, you can cut the second crust into strips and make a lattice crust on top. Bake as described above, until the crust is golden brown.

Epilogue

I find myself in a tricky position. I am a bread guy, and working with gluten has paid the bills for over twenty-five years. And, frankly, I love bread. However, although I'm not technically gluten intolerant, I totally accept the current data on the correlations between gluten and compromised health even for those who don't have celiac disease. Working with Denene and seeing the life and death aspects of diabetes and celiac disease was the motivation I needed to make a change. I have been overweight for twenty years, ever since I sold my bakery—where I burned off calories through hard physical work—to become a teacher and a writer. To further complicate matters, I report on the country's best pizza as the host of a website called Pizza Quest, which "requires" constant very tasty "research." Do you see my dilemma? I'm aware of the changes I should make to preserve my health, but putting them into action is difficult.

When I started working on this book with Denene, I weighed 214 pounds. Within two and half weeks of eating a low-carb diet while testing our recipes, I lost 14 pounds. Of course, I knew that the first pounds are the easiest to shed and that I couldn't keep up that pace but, hey, I'd settle for a pound a week. However, it wasn't long before the seesaw results of my twin projects became apparent. When I went back on the road to film a round of videos for Pizza Quest, I made my internal vows to eat sensibly and watch my carbs but the lure of the pizza siren was Homeric in its strength. The final weeks of editing, tweaking, and more recipe testing for this book were beneficial, but the gains were undercut by simultaneously teaching my artisan bread class at Johnson & Wales and consulting on a new pizza restaurant in Charlotte. I was stuck on the fulcrum of the seesaw.

Then Dr. Tom Schneider wrote his foreword for the book and I spoke with him about his own health transformations and the rationale behind the low-carb wellness movement. Again, I saw clearly that information is only part of the equation; it really comes down to will. So, once again, I decided to rededicate myself to modifying my eating habits, realizing that it would take a day-to-day effort to stick to the plan. I came to grips with the fact that, if I want to be able to eat a well-rounded diet that includes all the things I love, I must first restore my body to its proper healthy and functioning state. It hardly matters that I work out regularly and feel pretty good most of the time; the scale says I'm fifty pounds overweight and my body is storing too much of what I eat—even the healthy foods—as fat. That means I'm producing too much insulin and overworking my pancreas, wearing out my system and putting myself at risk. So, at the eleventh hour, in early January 2012, I rededicated myself to using these recipes as tools to rebuild my health. This is not a weight plan book—I used other resources to help me as well—but that was Day One of connecting the dots and gaining control of my eating.

As I write these words, I can give only a short-term progress report and can't promise that I will be able to stay the course. (Both Denene's story in the introduction and Dr. Schneider's Foreword illustrate the long-term results far better than mine.) I haven't cut out carbs completely, but try I to keep them to under 120 grams a day, and I reduced my sugar intake to about 15 grams a day, mainly from fruit. Within the first three days, I dropped 4 pounds (the easy ones). Better still, my energy level increased and I felt less drowsy after meals. I'm pleased to say that I'm keeping to the plan, continuing to eliminate excess carbs and using the recipes in this book every day to replace the usual breads and desserts I would have previously eaten. I have a couple of slices of our toasting bread everyday (toasted, of course)—it's my favorite! To confront my carb-heavy job, I take only small bites of students' bread to judge the quality. You can follow my progress at www.thejoyofgluten-freesugar-freebaking.com. My new life has begun.

Resources

Although there is no other book quite like this one, there have been a number of excellent gluten-free and diabetic friendly books that we've used as resources and that have paved the way for public acceptance and awareness. There is no way to list them all, but there are a few that we think you should consider for your own reference library. We list many on our website.

Gluten-Free

The Gluten-Free Almond Flour Cookbook and *Gluten-Free Cupcakes*, both by Elana Amsterdam (Berkeley, CA: Ten Speed Press)

The Allergen-Free Baker's Handbook by Cybele Pascal (Berkeley, CA: Ten Speed Press)

Gluten-Free Baking with The Culinary Institute of America by Richard J. Coppedge, Jr. (Avon, MA: Adams Media)

The Complete Idiot's Guide to Gluten-Free Cooking by Jean Duane (New York: Alpha Books)

Glutenology: Healthy Recipes for the Gluten-Free Warrior by Dr. Peter Osborne (Waverly, IA: G and R Publishing)

The Gluten-Free Gourmet Bakes Bread by Bette Hagman (New York: Henry Holt)

Diabetes and Glycemic Awareness

Glycemic Index Cookbook by Publications International, LTD (Lincolnwood, IL)

The GL Diet Made Simple by Antony Worrall Thompson (London: Kyle Books)

The Belly Fat Cure by Jorge Cruise (Carlsbad, CA: Hay House)

Death to Diabetes: The Six Stages of Type 2 Diabetes Control and Reversal by DeWayne McCulley (North Charleston, SC: Book Surge, LLC)

Dr. Neal Barnard's Program for Reversing Diabetes by Neal D. Barnard, MD (New York: Rodale)

Further Reading

There are many useful websites dedicated to both gluten intolerance and diabetes awareness, and an Internet search will lead you to them. These have been especially helpful to us:

www.celiaccentral.org: The official site of The National Foundation for Celiac Awareness.

www.celiac.com: One of the longest running websites dedicated to gluten intolerance.

www.glutenfreesociety.org: Dr. Peter Osborne's passionate site, which highlights many little known, hidden sources of gluten and the way gluten intolerance manifests even for those without celiac disease.

www.diabetes.org: The official site of The American Diabetes Association.

www.nal.usda.gov/fnic/foodcomp/search: A helpful database that provides nutrient information for a vast array of foods, allowing you to calculate the glycemic load.

www.nutritionvalue.org: Another great resource for information on the nutritional value of many ingredients.

www.floridahealthspan.com: Dr. Tom Schneider's medical institute focusing on wellness and regenerative medicine, with a special focus on diabetes and gluten awareness.

Sources and Manufacturers

The online retailer Netrition (**www.netrition .com**, (888) 817-2411) offers the best prices we've seen on all types of nut and seed flours and meal, liquid stevia, powdered stevia, ChocoPerfection bars, xanthan gum, baking powder, soy milk, rice milk, coconut milk, sugar-free maple syrup, and much more. Their flat shipping rate of $4.95 helps keep costs down.

Here are additional details on the individual brands and ingredients that we find perform the best in our recipes:

Aloha Nu
Coconut flour (It has the consistency of powdered sugar and works better than any other brand we've tried.)
www.simplycoconut.com • (888) 505-4439

Argo
Aluminum-free baking powder
www.argostarch.com • (866) 373-2300

Bob's Red Mill
Flax seed meal and whole flax seeds, hazelnut meal or flour, coconut flour, shredded unsweetened coconut flakes, garbanzo bean flour
www.bobsredmill.com • (800) 349-2173

Hershey's
Sugar-free chocolate syrup
www.thehersheycompany.com • (800) 468-1714

Honeyville Food Products
Our main source for almond flour and flax seed meal. (Purchasing in large quantities confers a price break.)
www.honeyvillegrain.com • (888) 810-3212

Low Carb Specialties
ChocoPerfection bars
www.chocoperfection.com • (800) 332-1773

NOW Foods
Sunflower seeds, liquid or powdered stevia, xanthan gum
www.nowfoods.com • (888) 669-3663

Maple Grove Farms
Sugar-free maple syrup, Vermont sugar-free syrup, sugar-free chocolate syrup
www.maplegrove.com • (802) 748-5141

Sensato
Powdered erythritol
www.sensatofoods.com

South Georgia Pecans
Our primary source for pecan meal, with the best price we've found.
www.georgiapecanstore.net • (800) 627-6630

WestSoy
Soy Slender vanilla or chocolate soy milk, unsweetened plain soy milk
www.westsoy.biz • (800) 434-4246

A Note on Bulk Bins and Store Brands

Bulk bins are usually the best option when purchasing nuts that you will grind into flour yourself, such as pecans, walnuts, sunflower seeds, sesame seeds, and others. Just check the stock to be sure the nuts are fresh—you want to buy from a store that moves through its bulk goods quickly. Individually packaged pecans in smaller amounts are likely to be quite a bit more expensive. Likewise, we use the generic brands of alternative sweeteners instead of always buying name-brand Splenda; they have the same formulation and perform at the same level, but are budget-friendly.

Acknowledgments

FROM PETER

This book would never have been possible without Denene Wallace, who has single-handedly pioneered the methods descibed in these pages. It was my good fortune to meet her at the right moment, just as the world was becoming more aware of the twin health crises of gluten intolerance and diabetes and their interconnectedness. Denene generously shared her methods with me and was a delight to partner with; she was a tireless worker as we crafted this book together over eighteen months.

Of course we both had tremendous support at home. As always, my wife, Susan, created the time and space necessary for me to carry my end. She was also a major contributor to the recipe-tweaking process, as she brought her objectivity and critical palate to the various tasting sessions. She is always the "secret weapon" behind my book and product development projects.

Thank you to Johnson & Wales University for again providing the flexibility that allowed me to work on this book, especially Charlotte campus president Art Gallagher, and the culinary and baking and pastry deans, Mark Allison and Wanda Cropper. Also, thanks to my colleague Laura Benoit, who provided her keen proofreading eye for the third book in a row.

This is my second collaboration with photographer Leo Gong, who proved again what a great talent he is as well as being a wonderful host. He and his wife, Harumi (and Samantha, their adorable mini-dachshund who was our team mascot for the second time), took great care of us during our weeklong photo shoot at their San Francisco studio. Karen Shinto again provided exceptional food styling and kitchen management support and I can't imagine accomplishing as much as we did in such a short time without her. Denene's mother, Dot, was amazing at the photo shoot, and many of the shots you see are a result of her contributions in the photo studio kitchen.

Thank you also to Melissa Moore, our super-talented and patient editor, who brought all the pieces together, and to the Ten Speed creative team, including designer Katy Brown and managing art director Betsy Stromberg. Many thanks to our copy editor Jasmine Star. This is my sixth book with Ten Speed Press and I don't believe there is a more creative, collaborative publishing house, so a special thanks to publisher Aaron Wehner, who has not only guided me through all of my Ten Speed books but who also conceived this one and invited me to take it on.

FROM DENENE

Without Peter's confidence in me I would not have been able to do this book. When Peter and I met a few years ago, he loved the taste of my recipes and graciously asked me to participate in this book. He is by far one of the most genuine people I know. His love for the art of baking great breads is contagious and I am proud to coauthor this book with him. Peter, thank you for believing in me.

It has been an honor to work with Ten Speed Press. Thank you all for making this a delightful experience.

My husband, Greg Wallace, is my rock. He has always helped me believe that I can do anything I choose. I love you with all my love.

My mom, Dot Miller, has been by my side in the kitchen for more than five years. Thank you for your time and support. And to my dad, John Miller, who taught me to "just keep pedaling," I love you both very much.

My niece and nephew, Lauren and Nicholas, have participated in more taste tests than I can count, providing me with very important feedback. Thank you both. You are the lights of my life.

It was obvious from the first time I met Dr. Tom Schneider that he truly gets it. Thank you, Tom, for being my friend and providing a wonderful and informative foreword to this book.

Dr. Tammy Robinson, my personal physician, taught me that I am brave and can manage my own health. Thank you for your dedication and compassion.

The following people have contributed in their own ways to making this book a reality. I am grateful for their friendships and I love each of you: Steve Avary, Mike and Kathy McGovern, Charles and Barbara Harvey, Herman Garner, Dr. Bruce McCormick, Octavia Shepard, Susan Reinhart, Melanie and J. T. Frazier, Ingrid and Paige Horil, Ginger Walker, Jennifer DeNyse, and many others.

My hope is that through small miracles like the recipes contained in this book, people all over the world can begin to heal their bodies. I am grateful on a daily basis for the healing I have experienced.

FROM PETER AND DENENE

Finally, a big, long thank-you to our many international recipe testers and Mark Witt, who coordinated the whole process by creating a dedicated Internet site and response mechanism that allowed us to merge all the feedback we received. The testing was absolutely critical in helping us make these recipes user-friendly, and especially important as we worked through all the variables regarding sugar replacements. Thank you all:

Stacy Abernathy, Patricia Alfano, Chuck Allen, Sandra Alvarez, Rohan Arnold, David Baldwin, Kristine Bertram, Barb Blackmore, Donna Bratton, Ricardo Brill-Thiel, Patricia Brogan, Sue Brogna, Kathryn Bundy, Patrick Campbell-Preston, Laurie Chappell, Nis'ku Closs, Mark Cohen, Kurt Congdon, David Coppes, Christopher Dana Benjamin DeKoven, Christopher Dibble, Louise Doubleday, Carolyn Doyle, Amy Dunbar-Wallis, Kevin Farnsworth, Tim Fischer, Richard Garay, Ofelia Gonzalez, Judith Griss, David Hellman, Jan Hickey, Annie Holt, Eirlys Jenkins, Carie Jo, Cindy Johansen, Kerry Johnson, Neal Johnson, Joyce Johnston, Robyn Josephs, Dan Kane, Julie Kato, Anne Kirkland, Logan Kistler, Norma Knepp, Donna Lamoreaux, Margie Layfield, Betty Lee, Johnisha Levi, Kristen Levitt, Jay Lofstead, Janice Mansfield, Monica Marty, Jeremy M. Matthews, Samantha Menzies, Gretchen Miller, Keila Miller, Andrea Morgan, Dan Morgan-Russell, Clark Murray, Jonathan Nacht, Trang Nguyen, Robert Nowacki, Jeanne Phillips, Marianne Preston, Sue Pye, Deborah Racine, Namita Reisinger, Norell Rosado, Steve J. Ross, Mary Ann Sereth, Audi Shake, Carole Sibley, Joseph Sloan, Jennet Sullivan, Dane Summers, Scott Thompson, Michelle Tseng, Tim Turmelle, Tanith Tyrr, Lasse Warje, Jacqueline Williams, and Michal Wolf.

Index